The New Other Woman

The New Other Woman

Contemporary Single Women in Affairs with Married Men

Laurel Richardson

THE FREE PRESS
A Division of Macmillan, Inc.
NEW YORK

The Free Press
A Division of Macmillan, Inc.
866 Third Avenue, New York, N.Y. 10022

Collier Macmillan Canada, Inc.

Printed in the United States of America

printing number

1 2 3 4 5 6 7 8 9 10

Library of Congress Cataloging-in-Publication Data

Richardson, Laurel Walum.
    The new other woman.

    Bibliography: p.
    Includes index.
    1. Single women—United States—Psychology.
2. Adultery—United States. 3. Mistresses—United
States. 4. Marriage—United States. I. Title.
HQ800.2.R53 1985   306.7'36   85–16261
ISBN 0–02–926890–7

*To
Ernest Lockridge*

Contents

Preface

A friend had been an Other Woman for almost two decades when her lover precipitately ended the relationship. Although she felt grief, loss, and displacement, there were few social supports for her and few sympathetic ears. She was socially stigmatized by mainstream society and ignored, at best, by the feminist one. She was the "other woman." Her experience was the initial impetus to do the research leading to this book—to the best of my knowledge, the first social-scientific analysis of the Other Woman. (Throughout this book I am referring to the subject of my research as the Other Woman while the designation the "other woman" refers to the cultural stereotype.)

For the following year or so, the idea of doing research on the contemporary Other Woman in the United States continued to intrigue me. Many single, and single again, women I knew or met or heard about were involved with married men. Being an Other Woman seemed to be emerging as a recognizable new social pattern for single women. Such relationships seemed to be fulfilling some major needs in the lives of a diverse population of women.

My research questions were many. They included specific questions about the structure of these relationships: Why does a single woman get involved with a married man? What does she expect to get from such a relationship? Who initiates the liaison? How is time spent together? How important is the sexual liaison to the woman? How does she handle her feelings about his wife? How does it affect her relationships with friends, family, and co-workers? How does it end, if it does? On balance, is this a "good" thing for a woman to do or not? I also had basic theoretical questions about the linkages between society and such relationships: What social and cultural factors facilitate these relationships, despite the social stigma? What will be their long-range social consequences on men, women, and the relationships between them?

My concern became twofold: To describe the experiences of the Other Woman and to provide a sociological analysis of relationships—not one-night stands—between single women and married men. Since there had been virtually no social-scientific research on the topic, I decided to interview Other Women.

Finding Other Women to interview was not difficult. Over a period of eight years—1977 to 1984—I traveled a great deal to attend conferences and to give public lectures. I announced my research interest to nearly everyone I met—conferees, salesclerks, travel acquaintances, and so on. Women I met in these different settings volunteered to be interviewed, or put me in contact with women who were involved with married men. In addition, many women over the course of the years of this research discussed some aspect of their relationship informally. Moreover, following news releases about the study, others wrote to me describing their relationships and/or asking to be interviewed. The material for this book came from all these sources, but primarily from in-depth interviews with 55 women who defined themselves as having, or having had, a long-term relationship with a married man.

Interviews took place in private settings—the respondent's home or mine, a hotel room, or occasionally a private office. They lasted between two and five hours and were tape-recorded and transcribed. I asked each woman to describe her feelings, expectations, and behavior before the relationship began, during its early stages, its mid-life, and its disintegration, if it had fallen apart. I also asked some general questions such as what advice she would give another single woman contemplating such a relationship and whether she would get involved again. The style and format of the interview elicited a great deal of information about the experiences of the single woman. It also evoked strong emotional responses. Many of the women cried at some point in the interview. Nearly all them thanked me for the "therapy" the interview provided, and several still phone me. (A copy of the interview guide is available in the Appendix.)

The women I interviewed ranged in age from 24 to 65, and resided in rural and urban areas in all regions of the country. When their relationships began, they ranged in age from 18 to 56, with a median age of 28. Fourteen women were high school graduates, 28 were college graduates, and 13 had advanced degrees. Occupationally, they were from all social strata and held a variety of blue collar, pink collar, and white collar—including administrative and professional—positions. Twenty-two of them had never been married, 33 of them had been. Twelve were raising children. For the most part, the men were older and better established than the women; 15 of the men had supervised or mentored the woman at some point during their relationship. When the relationships began, all of the husbands were living with their wives, and 45 of them had children living at home. Most of these relationships were over at the time of, or shortly after, the interview.

Because news of this research project was released to the press, I was contacted by women who were in the beginning stages of their liaisons. I interviewed seven of these women at approximately three-month intervals, longitudinally following the course of their relationships. Because these women's accounts were substantially consistent with the other interviews, the usual issues concerning the validity and reliability of retrospective biographies are muted.

Certain groups are not represented in the sample. For example, all the women in the sample were white. Based on exploratory interviews I did with a few women of color, the social context in which they are Other Women seemed different enough to give me pause. Women who had children with their married lovers are also not represented for similar reasons. And women who eventually married their married lovers are not included because none volunteered to be interviewed, and none in my longitudinal sample has married her lover. The generalizability of the study—as is true of nearly all studies—is therefore limited. Its validity, though, will rest, finally, in whether what I present resonates with the experiences of other Other Women.

I have written this book with two audiences in mind: the lay person and the professional sociologist. To make the material more accessible to the lay person, I have used few technical concepts and have introduced and elaborated various sociological ideas already familiar to the professional. In addition, I have made certain stylistic decisions. For example, I use the declarative mode almost exclusively. I also use the words "the Other Woman," rather than "the single women I interviewed involved with married men." But in order for the book to be of greater value to the sociological audience, I have done three things: I have referenced both empirical and theoretical sources relevant to the issue being discussed; I have indicated in the text, where appropriate, how the analysis may be relevant to understanding the construction of other nonnormative relationships; and I have attempted to blend older sociological perspectives with the newer sociological-feminist one.

In the process of doing this research, I have come to recognize how deeply ingrained are the normative judgments regarding the "other woman." I have had difficulty deciding what to call these women—indeed, what to name this book. The "other woman" has a pejorative ring, and linguistically asserts that the woman involved with a married man is "different," "expendable," the "outsider." Yet, that is how she has been viewed by the dominant society, and that view has shaped her experience. What I have done, after much internal debate, is to refer to all these women *collectively* as *Other Women* or the *Other Woman*. I have consciously chosen to claim the label and to capitalize their name. I do this to wrest it from its stigmatized context, and to remind the reader continuously that these women are not just "others" in the "some—; others—" grammatical construction: They are a distinct social group worthy of analysis. Single women involved with married men share a great deal in common; their lives and experiences have thus far been treated as *outside of* and *other than* the lives and experiences of "normal" women. But, as we shall see, the Other Woman's experiences have many parallels with the experiences of women, generally. In learning about the Other Woman we shall learn much about the lives, hopes, and problems of Everywoman.

Acknowledgments

Without the women who shared their lives with me, this book would not have been possible. So, first and foremost, I thank them. And without the help of the Ohio State University, colleagues, and friends this manuscript would still be in process. Some of the conceptual parts of this book were developed during a Faculty Professional Leave supported by The Ohio State University. The Department of Sociology provided some clerical and computer assistance. Several people read or discussed parts of this book at various stages of its writing: Nora Bawa, Howard Becker, Judith Cook, Roger Cooper, Joan Huber, Elaine Kerr, Betty Kirschner, Penelope Maza, and Elizabeth Menaghan. Their specialized expertise and input has been invaluable. Others—Lynn Atwater, Tim Diamond, Mary Margaret Fonow, Harriet Ganson, and Anne Statham—have read, critiqued, and discussed with me at length the entire manuscript at various stages of its development. That they gave so generously of their time and knowledge in the midst of their own demanding schedules is deeply appreciated. My editor at The Free Press, Joyce Seltzer, recognized the possibilities in the material and strongly urged me to look for its greater significance. Her energy and intelligence have been a constant inspiration. Everyone I came into contact with at The Free Press was helpful and highly competent. These included Karen Strauss, Edith Lewis, Louise Hochberg, and Ann Hirst. Lastly and most deeply, I thank Ernest Lockridge, who encouraged me to write this book, understood the difficulties involved, read each and every draft, and showed his caring in so many ways for both the writing and the writer.

Chapter One

THE OTHER
WOMAN
PHENOMENON

Beyond the primary world of husbands and wives, marriages and families, children and houses is another, second world, one shrouded in secrecy and stigma: the world of single women in long-term relationships with married men. There has been little social-scientific research on these relationships and virtually none from the perspective of the single woman. The contours of such relationships have been ignored, rendered invisible, and the women in them mute: the second sex in a second world.[1]

Relationships between single women and married men are by no means historically new, but there is something strikingly different about them today—they are ubiquitous. There is no doubt that the number of relationships between single women and married men has increased, and will continue to increase in the future.[2] In the 1980s, somewhere between 40 and 50% of married men report having had affairs and for those with incomes over $60,000, the figure rises to 70%. Over 15% of husbands report having a series of affairs. Today, men have affairs earlier in their marriages than they did twenty years ago, and nearly 70% of married men under age 40 imagine they will have an extramarital relationship.[3] Among the young adult population, there is greater acceptance of premarital and nonmonogamous sexual relationships. These are attitudes highly correlated with later permissiveness toward extra-marital sex.[4] Based on these facts, researchers' estimates predict that somewhere between one-half and two-thirds of husbands will have an extramarital liaison before the age of 40.[5] Who are the women they will get involved with? Although some of them will be married women, the majority are likely to be single women, because of the greater time and energy constraints on married women and the growing numbers of available unmarried women.[6]

The contemporary Other Woman is likely to be our neighbor, our sister, our daughter, our mother, ourselves: regular, normal, everyday single women. They are managers and workers, execu-tives and secretaries, professors and students, doctors and nurses. They come from all social strata. Many are women who, in an earlier era, would have recoiled at the murmur of an entanglement with a married man, but who, today, find a relationship with a married man acceptable.

One can neither ignore nor dismiss such a relationship as an individual aberration, because such relationships have become a way of life, a social pattern, for increasing numbers of single women. There is, today, a "new" Other Woman, and the phenome-non of single woman–married man liaisons is more and more wide-spread. As is true of any major new social pattern, it reflects the demographic, social, and cultural changes of the previous decade and portends the future as well.

Demographically, there are simply not enough single men for all the single women. One out of every five females does not have a potential mate. Currently, 40% of American women are single.[7] Due to the shortage of males, as well as to divorce, widowhood, and delayed marriage and remarriage, every woman is likely to be single for a substantial portion of her life.

For a single woman over the age of 25, there is a serious under-supply of available men, and as she ages that supply rapidly dimin-ishes: the older the woman, the strikingly fewer the men.[8] The shortage of men as women age is a result of the very large difference in mortality rates between the sexes, the high level of divorce in which divorced men remarry more frequently than divorced women, and men's preference for younger women.[9] For example, in 1980, widows outnumbered widowers six to one.[10] In 1983, there were 91 single divorced men for every 137 single divorced women.[11] Divorced men, ages 25–44, are twice as likely to remarry as divorced women in that age-group, while divorced men, ages 45–64, are four times as likely to remarry.[12] This leaves an ever-increasing number of women over 25 without potential marriage partners. For example, for every 223 unmarried women in their forties there are 100 unmarried men in their forties.[13] The men who are available draw from a wide range of women, including the pool of younger women.[14] Indeed, as men age, the penchant for younger and younger women increases, so that by the time men are in their forties, they are likely to marry women ten years their junior.[15] Should a women reenter singlehood in her late thirties or beyond, she is likely to remain single for the rest of her life.[16]

Looking at some of the social characteristics of the single male population decreases the number of eligible men even more. Nearly 14% of single men are homosexual, compared to an estimated 4% of women.[17] Moreover, the single men who are left tend to be those who are the least well-educated, least well-off, least well-situated occupationally, and most prone to mental and physical illnesses.[18] In 1980, 90% of highly educated, well-situated men were married.[19]

For the 33 million single women in America,[20] "a good man is hard to find." The more financially successful and highly educated the woman, moreover, the less likelihood she has of finding that "good man," since men tend to choose wives who are less well-educated and less financially successful than themselves. Our cultural preference is still strong for men to "marry down" and for women to "marry up"—so strong, in fact, that any single woman over 25 with a college education has reduced chances of ever getting married. In 1985, for every 10 women between 40 and 49 years of age with a college education, there are only 3 single men who are older and better educated available as potential mates.[21] Moreover, for that growing class of female executives and professionals, an elite class of women who have sought graduate training and achieved economic independence, there are very few men available. The "heiress problem"—how to find an appropriate husband in

a "sparsely stocked and heavily fished pool of men at the top"—
is now a problem for an entire class of women.[22]

Demographic realities have profound social-psychological
consequences for relationships between men and women. One of
the major consequences of the shortage of single men is that *all*
men—married and unmarried—acquire additional power in their
relationships with women. Because men have many possible alternative relationships, due to their sex being in short supply, their
dependency on any particular relationship is reduced. Even more
crucially, though, men's expectations of satisfaction within any
given relationship are heightened. If men are not satisfied, they
have other options.[23] Men do not have to be demographers to
know that they have this new advantage, the power to demand
satisfaction by threatening the termination of the relationship. As
a consequence, a man is more likely to resist commitment to a
particular woman and more likely to be involved with more than
one woman. So strong is this social-psychological outcome that
Barbara Ehrenreich has described the "hearts of men" as being
in a "flight from commitment."[24]

Women, on the other hand, because there are more of them,
have fewer options and more difficulty in finding a satisfactory
relationship. A shortage of men means that many women have
had, and will have, emotionally painful experiences with men, because when men are scarce they can demand more in a relationship
and be more cavalier and callous. Women are devalued because
there is an "excess" of them: "There's always another (newer, younger, fresher) apple in the barrel."

Although there are not enough men to go around, the old and
deep cultural imperative persists: A woman should be in a relationship with a man in order to be a regular, normal, attractive woman.
Few women can escape the imprint of socialization for heterosexual
couplehood. From childhood on, parents, peers, and the media rein-
force definitions of femininity and womanliness, worth and desir-
ability, that are intricately linked to being in a heterosexual
relationship.[25] Having the love of a man is probably the single
most compelling demand placed upon a woman by herself and
her society. It is the female equivalent of the male injunction to

achieve financial success. Contemporary single women are, consequently, placed in an untenable position: there are not enough "available" men; yet, unless they "have" a man they are not "normal" women.

Generally, when people lack the socially approved means to achieve a culturally desirable goal, they find alternative ways to attain it. These ways may be seen as innovative, pioneering, or deviant.[26] Given the demographic constraints, many single women who accept the goal of heterosexual couplehood will have to turn to socially disapproved ways to achieve it. One such way is a relationship with a married man.

There are some other alternatives for heterosexual single women: dating much younger men, dating much older men, dating gay men, communal living, celibacy, or lesbianism. But these are not only less common solutions, they are probably less viable. Younger men typically prefer younger women; older men are mostly married or otherwise unavailable; one's self-image, sexual satisfaction, and sexual self-esteem are undermined by socializing almost exclusively with gay men; and few opportunities are available for communal living. Single women can choose, of course, as many do, to opt out of the male market—to become celibate or lesbian.[27] These choices, however, if taken by a heterosexual woman as a "second-best," or as a forced compromise, or if not chosen at all, but happened into, can leave the woman with nagging questions and unresolved issues: Where is *my* man? Am I a "normal" woman? On the face of it, then, relationships with married men offer one of the more *viable* alternatives for heterosexual single women.

The married man solution is thinkable, however, for large numbers of women only because the women's and sexual liberation movements have had a major impact on the consciousness of single women. The feminist movement of the seventies has changed the attitudes of contemporary women concerning their place in society and the economy.[28] For example, according to a 1984 Harris Poll, 74% of U.S. women believed they were not getting equal pay for equal work, in contrast to 19% in 1971; 63% believed they were discriminated against in promotion, compared to 29% in

1971.[29] In their 1982 study and review, *Singles: The New Americans,*
Jacqueline Simenaur and David Carroll estimate that three-quarters
of single American women hold feminist tenets.[30]

Over the past decade and a half, moreover, females have grown
increasingly liberal in their sexual attitudes and behavior—so liberal
that at this point there is a convergence toward a single premarital
sex standard for both men and women.[31] In contrast to 1965, for
example, when 70% of college women (who were virtually all
single) viewed sex outside of marriage as immoral, only 20% did
a decade later[32]—a percentage that has persisted into the present.[33]
The rates of coitus have similarly accelerated for women. Between
1971 and 1976, for example, there was a 30% increase in the number
of nonvirginal women under the age of 19.[34] Although only 25%
of single college women had sexual intercourse in the 1940s, that
percentage had almost tripled by the 1980s.[35] Since autonomy from
parental control is a primary factor in having sex outside of marriage, we would expect the population of adult single women—
most of them living alone, with roommates, or heading families
of their own—to be sexually active women.[36]

Alongside traditional beliefs, then, are new ones proclaiming
a woman's right to economic and career success, her right to her
own body, her right to experiment sexually, her right to define
her own lifestyle, and her right to name herself and her experiences.
As a result, the contemporary woman has new expectations for
herself and her relationships. She expects to be more independent
in her thinking and more successful in her career. She imagines
she is entering a world of nearly unlimited opportunities, where
her possibilities for growth and experience are ever-expanding.
With an increasing number of female role models in managerial
and professional positions, her emergent belief that she has some
control over her personal destiny is strengthened. With greater
confidence in herself, her abilities, and her future, she enters the
public sphere without regrets or self-recriminations about her desire
for career success.

These feelings of personal efficacy in an ever-widening sphere
of career opportunity are carried over into women's beliefs that
they can have some control over and independence in their relationships with men. Seeing themselves as active participants in the

social and economic worlds, they imagine they will be able to determine as well where love and intimacy will fit into their lives. Intimate relationships which may have appeared "risky" to previous generations of women now appear "safe," because contemporary women see themselves as having control over the direction, intensity, and duration of the relationship.

But feminist consciousness is not all of a piece, nor does it guarantee that others will treat one as one wishes to be treated. Consequently, women are in a paradoxical situation. On the one hand, they are embracing new liberated roles while, on the other, their socialization, sex-stereotyping, and patriarchal institutions continue to constrain them. Tensions and personal ambivalences result.[37]

One of the primary tensions in contemporary women's lives is the problem of achieving both an independent identity and a satisfying intimate relationship. In earlier eras, a woman's identity was placed "on hold" until she knew who her husband would be. The aphorism, "you do not marry the man, you marry his life," was essentially true. A woman became Mrs. Man's First and Last Name and lived out her female destiny through her husband and children. Indeed, the plot of most women's novels for several centuries has been the quest for a man's love; through marriage both intimacy and an identity are achieved. The novel climaxes with the heroine transformed into a bride, her aimlessness over, her worth recognized.[38]

The romance novel still sells well, but increasingly women question the peculiarity of a social script that requires them to "choose another so as to choose a self."[39] Modern women are struggling with the problem of whether it is possible, much less desirable, to achieve identity and intimacy simultaneously. Many wonder, given the power imbalances between men and women and the differences in their socialization, whether a woman can maintain her identity as a separate self while in an intimate relationship with a man. And if she can, at what cost? So much of her socialization has been to defer to, to make amends for, to please, or to accept a man's definitions of situations that often enough she finds herself feeling guilty if she asserts herself and resentful if she does not.

For a modern woman to find her way and her own identity is no easy task. In our world nearly any aspect of one's selfhood can be perused and altered: body shape, psychological states, sexual orientation, educational level, occupational choice, family roles. Never have there been so many options for women.

Choosing and pursuing these new options, however, requires unencumbered *time:* time to think, study, achieve, be autonomous. Many women fear that marriage, or even a highly committed relationship with an available man, will distort and prematurely waylay their quests, because relationships are demanding and time-consuming.[40] For a woman to achieve occupational success, for example, at the same time she is trying to create a lasting relationship, means she is likely to experience considerable strain when the inevitable conflicts over time, energy, and loyalty between her career and her love arise.[41] Similarly, a divorced mother may experience overload if she tries to earn an income, raise her children, and build a relationship with an agreeable father for them who is also a suitable husband for her.

Today, then, the demographics and socialization toward heterosexual couplehood, combined with women's need for time to achieve new goals and solve new problems, make the acceptance of a relationship with a married man more likely. Since women have greater expectations for themselves, new and broader life agendas, and greater economic success in careers, the urgency and priority that "getting" married once had in a woman's life has been lessened. Believing she can stay in control in her relationship while she accomplishes other goals, a single woman is both pushed and pulled into liaisons with married men.

Because many women are adopting new roles, they may believe that a temporary relationship with a married man will fit into their lives. One of the major new roles that women are choosing is that of student. The majority of undergraduates are women, many of them returning older women, and their predominant marital status is single. Nearly 50% of the master's degrees and 30% of the doctoral degrees since 1974 are being awarded to women, and the number of women in professional programs, such as law and medicine, has quintupled in the last decade.[42] For these women, getting an education is a primary goal, one that may preclude a permanent marital relationship in the foreseeable future.

University education prepares women for another new role—high-powered professional and managerial careers. In 1983, 33% of administrative and managerial positions were held by women.[43] Many women are measuring their success by the traditional masculine yardsticks of occupational position, upward mobility, financial remuneration, authority, and prestige. Holding heightened expectations turns professional and managerial careers into more than full-time jobs, because success often requires 60 or 70 work hours a week. When the emotional and power issues that face women at work, such as finding a suitable mentor, fears of failure, fears of success, and sexual harassment, are added together, women do not have a lot of time or energy left for building a "regular" relationship with a man.

Many women today, then, are forging new identities through education and careers. They define themselves independently of having found "Mr. Right." They see themselves as complete in and of themselves, rather than as heroines in a Jane Austen novel, who become all they can be by marrying. But equally important, they are struggling to redefine what intimacy between a man and a woman can and should feel like. The old marriage plot, the old division of labor between the sexes, the old dominant man–submissive woman psychological patterns, are more than old: they are painful, even oppressive.

Because these demographic, sociological, and cultural realities affect all women, women from diverse backgrounds, with diverse interests and goals, get involved with married men. Moreover, given that these realities will not disappear in the near future, it is likely that the single woman over 25 who has never had a relationship with a married man will be in the minority. Many liaisons will last for months and years; some for decades.

Despite the social forces tending to shape the "new" Other Woman, cultural stereotypes persist. These judgments label Other Women as economically parasitical, psychologically sick, and sociologically deviant.[44] Least insidious, although not a wholly innocent caricature, is the popular image of the Other Woman as a "kept" woman. According to this fantasy, the Other Woman is a very attractive woman who provides her married lover with sexual favors and companionship in exchange for luxurious housing, food, and clothing. Although very few Other Women live in this way, the stereotype serves to divert attention from the material realities of their lives and from the ways in which their existences are ordinary and similar to those of "regular" women. Other Women come from all social strata, and for the most part work to support themselves; they are not "kept."[45]

More damaging is the stereotype of the Other Woman as psychologically sick. There are two distinct versions of this: the masochistic woman and the narcissistic child.[46] According to the masochistic woman version, the Other Woman repeatedly seeks pain. The roots of the masochism, it is argued, rest in her infancy and childhood. Perhaps she was an abused child. Whatever, she learned to associate pain with love. Now, as an adult, she purposefully seeks painful relationships, for that is the only way she can feel loved.

The narcissistic child version purports that the Other Woman has never resolved her Electra complex—the female equivalent of the Oedipus complex. She still wants to be Daddy's little girl, and so is neurotically compelled to compete with her mother by going after another woman's husband. In her most neurotic form, she seeks revenge against all women who have husbands, which, in her distorted mind, means they have won Daddy's love. Willfully, then, the mistress sets out to be a homewrecker, to break up other people's marriages, because she was so woefully unable to break up her own parents' marital bond. Because she could not steal away her Daddy, she will "husband steal" instead.

Although any given Other Woman probably knows that she is neither more nor less masochistic or narcissistic than "regular" women, nevertheless she is probably troubled by the grain of truth that does apply to her, and sometimes in bad moments envisions that grain as a bushel. And even though many psychologists have rejected the diagnosis of female masochism and narcissism as either applicable to both men and women or not applicable at all, the image of the Other Woman as a neurotic that dominates the media is difficult to ignore.

By labeling women involved with married men as parasitical, sick, and deviant, we create a class of women who are viewed as different from the rest of their sex; an embarrassment to regular women; misfits; women who are destined to have a socially marginal kind of life. The label becomes a blinder: we see neither the actual experience of the Other Woman, nor how our contemporary world has spawned and structured the second one. Ideological and intellectual complacency follow. By dividing women into the kept and the free, the sick and the well, the deviant and the normal, based on the social legitimacy of their relationships to men, we etch male-centered values even more deeply into our consciousness. Women, who are traditionally defined by their relationship to a man, have their identities subordinated and their lives separated from each other. Other Women remain the other *than,* the different *from,* the outside *of.*

Yet, in many respects, the Other Woman is an ordinary woman—a woman experiencing the same stresses, pushes, and pulls that regular women experience. The lives of the women upon whom this book draws testify to that. These are 55 women who came from different social strata and who are beautiful, pretty, and plain; stylish, nondescript, and unkempt; assertive and reticent; funny and serious; religious and nonreligious; politically conservative and politically liberal; feminist activists and more traditional. Educationally, they have high school diplomas, college degrees, and advanced professional degrees. Occupationally, they run the gambit from unskilled to skilled workers to professionals and executives, both salaried and self-employed. By looking at the lives of Other Women within contemporary society, one can learn much about the lives of all women.[47] To know about the contemporary Other Woman is to know more about the hopes and conflicts of every woman. And to know how their relationships with married men are constructed is to know more about the character and consequences of male-female relationships, in general, and about the future of friendship, sex, and love between women and men.

In a world where there are not enough men, but where a persistent cultural imperative demands that women be heterosexually coupled to feel good about themselves, and in a world where women are restricted by the demands of social convention and pulled by new opportunities, being with a married man seems to be a genuine solution. Because all single women are constrained by the same pressing demographic and cultural realities, the Other Woman phenomenon is ubiquitous.

Ubiquity, however, does not necessarily mean that such relationships are good—nor for that matter, that they are bad. But it does mean they are fulfilling a larger social as well as personal function that bears closer analysis. Is a relationship with a married man, in practice, beneficial or costly to the single woman? Is being involved with a married man, in actuality, a viable solution for a single woman? What does this phenomenon portend for the future of relationships between women and men and relationships between women and women? To answer these questions, we begin at the beginning: how single women and married men get involved.

Chapter Two

GETTING INVOLVED

SINGLE WOMEN do not set out to "husband steal" or even to "husband borrow." Yet, every setting and every occasion in which married men and single women meet are potential places and times for a relationship to begin. Due to the increased number of single women in social and work settings, single women and married men are frequently meeting, talking, and interacting. The sheer number of such interactions increases the probability of some of them becoming more intimate relationships.

Although many single women find that there are no single men available, or that the ones available are of "poor quality," few *plan* on turning to married men as an alternative. They do not consciously *choose* to become Other Women. Indeed, most explicitly deny premeditation:

I would never calculate to have an affair with a married man.

I never intended to get involved.

I was into my celibate period. I wasn't interested in men, much less a married one.

> After my husband left me for an "other woman," I told
> myself I would never, never do that to another woman.

The theme is so persistent that it cannot be dismissed: single
women, by and large, do not see themselves as husband poachers.
It is likely that most husbands would also deny that they are hunt-
ing for single women.[1] If neither the married male nor the single
female sees him- or herself as purposefully seeking a liaison—if
we cannot attribute their involvement to conscious, individual mo-
tives—then, why does it happen? How do married men and single
women get together?

In our society, being aware of and responding to the sexuality
of the other, either consciously or unconsciously, is the way in
which males and females have learned to relate to each other. Even
in nonerotic settings, male-female interaction is continuously influ-
enced by the other person's sex.[2] Encounters between a man and
a woman, no matter how incidental, have an underlying sexual
element. Although this element may be suppressed, ignored, or
otherwise not acted on, as is usually the case, nevertheless, it is
still there. This is one of the consequences of living in a culture
with a strong heterosexual imperative—what Adrienne Rich refers
to as "compulsory heterosexuality."[3] Almost unconsciously, the
participants evaluate each other's sexual attractiveness.[4] The attraction is justified, after the fact, by imputing traits already valued
by one to the other.[5]

People explain feelings of attraction by saying the other person
makes them feel good about themselves. A man is more likely to
feel good about himself in the presence of a woman if he believes
she finds him sexually attractive; a woman is more likely to feel
good about herself in the presence of a man if she believes he
likes and respects her as a person, not "just a sex object." Men
and women usually use different criteria, then, to interpret their
attraction. The man will probably want to prove she is, in fact,
sexually interested in him, whereas the woman will probably want
to prove that he is interested in her as a person, not just as a sex
object. For men, then, the distinction between being sociable and
being sexual is blurred, while for women it is sharpened.[6]

According to the regular heterosexual norms governing the first encounter between a man and a woman, either the male or the female may show initial interest. If the woman initiates, however, the cues are to be subtle, such as eye contact or asking for a light. These the man can *interpret* as sexual interest in him, even though she may simply want to see him better or only want a light. According to our sexual-social norms, he can now legitimately take the initiative, although in these early exchanges she retains the right to terminate the encounter. If she does not rebuff his advances, he can conclude that she is attracted to him and available *to him.*

The idea of availability is an important factor in the man's evaluation of the situation. Single women, simply by virtue of being single, are considered available in a way that married women are not. Because a married woman "belongs" to another man, unless she gives strong cues to the contrary, she will be assumed to be taken. To assume the contrary is to court disaster in the form of her outraged husband. The risks to ego and body are too great. Because many men do view married women as "belonging" to another man, even if they do give off cues of availability, they may be ignored because a man wants to avoid potential trouble with her husband.[7]

In the world of single women and married men, though, the threat of violence between men over a woman is lessened. Men can continue to initiate those encounters, as they always have. But, something else is happening today as well. There are increased numbers of single women in diverse settings who take the initiative in their interactions with men. For the most part, women intend these interactions as simply sociable or professional, but men can interpret them as sexual. For example, a woman may ask a man for information, request his help, or tell him how independent she is—statements which she intends at face value, not as sexual come-ons. He may interpret her request for knowledge, her plea for help, or her declaration of independence as proof that she is making herself available to him. His interpretation, moreover, is not totally ill-founded, because although she may not be trying to lure him, she probably does find him, if not attractive, at least not repugnant. Moreover, she is single. Unless a single woman desexualizes herself by layering her body with heavy, ill-fitting clothing or fat, she represents erotic potential. Should she continue the exchange, he is further convinced that his interpretation is correct, for the more he learns about her as a woman in transition, a woman open to new experiences, a "liberated woman," or, conversely, a woman in need, a woman in trouble, the more "data" he has to support his assumption about her availability. On her part, because she wants to believe she is respected for herself, she downplays the impact of her sexuality on him. Moreover, because he is married, she can interpret his interest in her as nonsexual:

> I didn't read the cues. I was just totally unaware of it. Which, by the way, never happened with single men, because I'm looking for it with them. I see them as potentials.

For the most part, then, neither the married man nor the single woman is purposefully engineering an involvement but, unwittingly, the regular rules of heterosexual attraction and availability are prevailing as more single women increase their social and professional activities and go about the process of changing their lives.

Change casts women into transitional roles—going back to school, getting divorced, getting new jobs, reexamining their old identities. Indeed, one of the primary characteristics of contemporary women's lives is the transitional nature of their circumstances. The changeable nature of their lives plays a major role in their getting involved with married men: whenever people are unsettled and in-between they are susceptible to new experiences. Many single women are going through role or personal transitions when they meet a married man:

> I was returning to school after a fifteen-year hiatus. I was nervous and excited.

> My husband had left me for another woman, and I was struggling to get my self-esteem back.

> I was just starting out as a lawyer.

I wanted to find out who I was.

I was working out whether I could be heterosexual or not.

Because there are so many more options for women today than previously, the potential kinds of changes are many: educational, career, marital, or sexual preference. There are few role models in life or fiction to emulate, though, and no "how-to" book in the face of an increasingly strident cultural demand that a woman "find herself." Women who have gone through a major transition, moreover, may be dissatisfied with where that passage has led. But unlike women living in earlier eras, contemporary women see that their lives can change over and over again; their destiny is not eternally constrained by their previous decisions. New roles and new relationships are always possible.

Because there are new roles and new activities for single women, the numbers and kinds of places where they may meet married men have enlarged. Today, single women meet married men in the daily rounds of their lives, through work, and through leisure-time activities. With so many single women in the labor force, they frequently meet married men through their work. Because women, however, are still clustered in low-paying, low-prestige positions, the married men they meet at work tend to be their occupational superiors:

I went in for an interview, and it was really a sharp job. It was a $5000 promotion and I was going to go into management, no more clerical. I knew I could do it, but I didn't have any background to prove it. He would be my boss. He was just a neat person, and we talked, but it was all above board.

I had taken a couple of classes from him and I had done well in them and I had decided to concentrate in his area. I became his research assistant.

Most women have been and will continue to be occupationally subordinated to men, and, consequently, meeting married men who are their superiors is well institutionalized. Because women see powerful men as desirable, on the one hand, and because their jobs often depend upon compliance with their supervisor's wishes, on the other, additional, strong social forces are at work facilitating a liaison.[8]

In addition to the well-established work pattern of male bosses and female subordinates, a new trend is the entrance of women into male-dominated occupations as colleagues. Since the male occupational world has been one where "male bonding" has been accomplished through the exclusion of women, their entrance has been resisted. One of the major rationalizations for keeping women out of the man's work world has been the assumption that with their entry will come sexuality, jealousy, and dissension: men's minds will be taken off their work and male solidarity will be threatened.[9]

Whether the woman is sexually attractive or not, however, is less important than the fact that beliefs have real consequences—what Robert Merton has referred to as the "self-fulfilling prophecy."[10] If men see women essentially as sexual beings, even in nonsexual settings, then they will cast them into sexual roles. If women's sexuality is salient in work settings, they are continuously responded to and judged by sexual criteria which distort their perceived competence and increase the potential for actual liaisons between single women and married men.[11] Because there are few clear rules about how men and women "act" when they are equals, there is even confusion about how to interpret the good feelings associated with colleagueship:

> We were both research interns and were interviewing community leaders together. He wasn't competitive or arrogant. He wasn't always putting me down and making me feel stupid. And I didn't feel like he was trying to get me into bed. I didn't know how to interpret it. I'd never had a working relationship with a man before.

So strong is the underlying heterosexual eroticism of the culture that a face-to-face meeting is not even necessary for a work liaison to begin, as witnessed by the experience of a woman editor with a married male author, her eventual lover. They "met" through their work computer system, and initially they communicated exclusively through the computer:

> I met him on-line. We worked together through computer conferencing. I liked how his mind worked. Then one day he called me [on the computer] on the personal mode—that way no one else can read the message. I was flattered that he approached me because I had this mental picture of him as someone important. So we started chatting on-line. I thought an electronic flirtation would be safe.

In addition to meeting married men through one's work, single women may meet them through their leisure time and social activities. However, because singles and couples are socially segregated and because most leisure-time activities are organized around same-sex groups,[12] relationships that begin through a shared social life are relatively uncommon. An unattached single woman, moreover, is particularly unwelcome in the coupled world because she is seen as a threat. So unless a married man attends singles' functions or goes to "regular" social functions without his wife, a liaison beginning through one's social life is unlikely. This is not to say that relationships never begin socially. After a woman is divorced, she might establish a new relationship with an "old friend":

> We had all been couple friends before the divorce. Afterwards [after her divorce], he'd drop by and help me with the yard and stuff. He tuned my car, and we'd talk. He was a good and old friend.

Nor is it to say that a mutual friend might not facilitate an introduction:

> I had a divorced, male friend who had an interior design business in the village where I lived. We were sitting in

Jerry's, and he told me about his partner and what a sad case that was. He [the partner] was really unhappily married, but he just wanted some women friends. I said, "Well, you should invite him along with us the next time." I thought that was dumb of me—you don't even want to meet this person. But then I dropped into the store and I met him, and I was very aware of his presence, and he went with us to Jerry's.

Male bonding has a long history, and the man who "stands in" for another man is not only legendary ("Speak for yourself, John") but common enough to have its slang word, the "beard." From junior high school on, boys and then men pander for one another; male bonding is accomplished through the vicariously or actually shared bounty. In a coterie of divorced men with buddy-ship ties to married ones, the potentialities are many. The divorced man can play the "beard," taking care of his pal's need for a woman's friendship.

In addition to meeting through work or social life, single women meet married men accidentally. For women with high-status careers, the opportunities for chance encounters are many since their work takes them into diverse settings, increasing the types and frequency of casual interchanges. But virtually all single women have greater freedom of movement today than formerly, making serendipitous meetings relatively frequent:

He was my seatmate [on the airplane]. We started talking, and I was telling him about my nervousness about returning to school, and it turned out he was a professor at the university, and he seemed so supportive. He was very helpful and reassuring. Confidence-building. It turned out we had the same destination.

I was bound and determined to get my bod in shape. I was feeling fat and flabby and disgusted with myself. Anyway, "Coach," as I started to call him, came up to me while I was dissolving on the Nautilus and asked if I wanted some help. He got me on a workout schedule when he was there, too. We'd sit in the whirlpool and talk.

I was restless bored and I went into a bar I had never been in before. I was just drinking and talking to some old man when this clown started nibbing into the conversation. I wasn't even planning to meet anyone when he got up and said to me, "Are you coming?" And I said "No." And he said, "I'll wait for you outside"—sort of like he lured me out of the bar with him. Just to spend the night—one of those easy kind of things.

For each of these women, and others like them, the sexual liberation and feminist movements have brought them into settings that used to be primarily male—airplanes, gyms, bars. Moreover, these social movements have made it possible for women to talk to men in those settings, to share cabs and whirlpools, and even to share beds as "an easy kind of thing." It is as though women's independence has overturned the parental admonition: the grown daughter talks to strangers.

Talking to strangers, moreover, especially for a single woman going through a major life transition, is a salutary activity. With a stranger she can briefly practice her new role; she can act differently. Because for the most part she will find these brief encounters with strangers pleasant, healing, and instructive, she is likely to initiate more of them and to be more responsive and experimental within them.[13] The sheer number of such seemingly insignificant encounters which are experienced as positive therefore is likely to increase, and thus the potential for new liaisons also increases.

Between work, play, and the simple business of getting through one's daily life, as well as the more complex matter of going through major role transitions, opportunities for unexpected encounters between single women and married men are many. That they meet each other is not surprising. Since we live in a culture which eroticizes interactions between males and females, neither is it surprising that these encounters have a sexual component. But these do not explain how it is that single women and married men become more involved; how friendly, casual, or work relationships are transformed into intimate ones. One of the primary reasons these relationships escalate is because men and women have different assessments of the situation: "His" reality and "her" reality are not the same.[14]

Few single women think the married man is interested in them because they are *women*. Few think they are "sex objects" or even "sex persons" to their eventual lover, in their initial encounter. Rather, the single woman constructs a fairly commonplace, routine explanation for why he is showing interest in her. She casts him in a familiar, nonthreatening role: old friend, new friend, mentor, colleague, or temporary encounter. Even the occasional woman who sees the man as a sexual possibility casts him in the safe role of a "casual," a one-night stand, not a lover. Whatever a woman's definition of the relationship, she thinks her definition is mutually shared; the relationship seems safe.

Part of the reason she believes the relationship is safe is because the man rarely hides his marital status:

He was wearing a wedding band.

He had a picture of his wife and kids on his desk.

His wife worked for the company too, and periodically she'd bop in and out.

So intent can a single woman be on defining the situation as a neutral one and their relationship as something "above board," that even when deceived about his marital status, she may justify continuing the relationship because she believes her definition will control its subsequent development:

It was a couple of weeks after we had met at the bar and had gotten together a couple of times that I asked him if he had ever been married, and he said, "yes." I took that to mean he was presently divorced.

I didn't feel tricked, although I felt a little put out that
he hadn't told me [he was still married]. I guess I was a
little disturbed, but I didn't have any strong feelings for
him at that time, and I was interested in someone else, and
I thought, well, he could be a friend.

One of the primary realities, though, that women do not recognize is that their definitions of situations, meanings, and intentions
differ from men's: The words they use are the same, but the meanings those words convey are not.[15]

Friendship is one of those *gendered* words that has different
meanings to women and to men. For women, friendship means
being vulnerable, open, self-disclosing, and emotionally supportive.
For men, friendship is doing things together, hanging out. From
childhood on, differences in friendship patterns between males and
females are common. Young girls tend to have exclusive twosome
friendships with emotional intimacy, whereas young boys tend
to be together in groups, on teams, or in gangs, with limited emotional sharing. As the children grow into adolescence, they enlarge
their circle of friends—but girls still tend to be in smaller cliques
than boys, and to define friendship as confiding and conversation
rather than doing things together, which the boys define as
friendship.[16]

Emotionally intimate friendships are important to women, and
women want men to be friends. Single women cast married men
into the role of "old friend" or "new friend." "Old friends" are
familiar and safe. For example, a woman who had known her eventual married lover since college thought it "only natural" that he
should help her with the heavy work around the house following
her divorce. After he had cleaned the gutters or mowed the lawn,
they would eat lunch and drink beer and "talk about old times.
Real good friends." She concealed her increasing affection for him,
by labeling him an "old friend."

Women also commonly view the initial phase of their relationships with married men as new friendships. New acquaintances
are cast into the role of "new friends":

I thought he was an interesting guy and would make a nice friend.

He was so kind to me. He really seemed to care about me the way friends do.

It was a time in my life when I needed a friend, and he was it.

However, because the sexual element is present, even if suppressed, the sexual tension of remaining "just friends" with someone she finds attractive can surface:

We talked about it [the relationship] for several months, and I only saw him after work. I told him I wouldn't mind just being friends, purely platonic, but if he wanted a flesh relationship, forget it. Because he kept seeing me, I knew he wanted to be friends too.

Proof that he is a friend rests on his willingness to forego a sexual liaison. Obviously, though, the idea of a sexual relationship had been raised, verbally or nonverbally, for otherwise she would have had no need to discuss it with him. Less obviously, that she was willing to discuss it for several months means that enough time was invested for her to believe there was a friendship, albeit a friendship that was sliding over into something more:

We didn't see each other for two months. I thought he was getting too interested, and I didn't want to get involved with a married man, because I always told myself I would never do this, never, never. I was attracted to him, and so I was telling him how I felt about these kinds of involvements, and telling myself, too. At that point, we were just good friends, and I didn't think that was harmful. He was fun to be with and comfortable, and he seemed intelligent.

Her ambivalence is showing. She sees their relationship as "just good friends," but is concerned that he is "too interested" and that she is "attracted" to him. She really does know that he is no longer "just fun and comfortable to be with"; she really does know that he is a potential lover. She decides to back off from him for a while.

This woman's struggle to maintain the definition of the situation as a friendship is repeated by many single women. But even if they succeed, they may eventually lose because friendship is so often viewed by women as a preamble to sex and love, an issue that will concern us much more later.

Sexual tensions that arise with male friends, then, can create problems for women. But, if one is experiencing those tensions with one's boss or co-worker, the problem is even more severe because the woman's job may be at stake. One way to reduce the tension is to cast the man firmly into the role of supervisor, mentor, or colleague. Since work roles are interdependent and since work is accomplished through *social* interaction, men and women are together, formally and informally. At the office, the university, the hospital, the mill, and so on, the married man is the single woman's boss, mentor, or colleague. Work roles *explain* for the single woman, in the beginning, why the married man is in her life:

We were on the same committee.

He was my advisor.

He was my direct supervisor.

He worked at the studio too. He was a director.

Propinquity increases the need to reduce tensions and abort conflicts. Therefore, most single women want to discount any suspicion they may have that more than work, mentoring, or collegiality is going on. For most single women, because they do not want to call the men around them sexual harassers, it is almost imperative

to deny or minimize the sexual overtones. This is not to say that
all women are unaware of their sexual attractiveness or that none
of them enjoy the feelings of power that this gives them. Nor is
it to say that no women choose consciously to trade on their sexual
attractiveness. It is to say, though, that women, by and large, under-
estimate the impact of their sexuality in their working relationships
with men.[17] The experience of a young executive is illustrative:

> Occasionally, our whole unit would go for drinks or some-
> thing, but it was all of us as a group. Then, I became the
> senior manager in the office, and I started having business
> lunches with him. Those were very professional, if anything
> overly so. But the group, still, would go out and socialize.
> We'd go to Shadows [a disco]. He and I would talk and
> dance. After a while, he'd call and say, "Come over to Shad-
> ows and we can play backgammon and discuss . . ." For
> me, it was like one more male mentor.

Socializing with her boss began easily, harmlessly as the whole
unit went together. Twosome business lunches followed, as well
as continued group socializing, discos, and dancing. Before long,
only she and her boss were meeting at the disco. She insisted,
however, that his interest, at that point, was only in her executive
potential. She refused to acknowledge that a disco was an odd
setting for business discussions. "He chose it," she said, "because
he knew it was close to my apartment," as though that were a
business decision on his part, rather than, as it turned out, "a
sexual opportunistic one."

Women expect that male friends and workmates will be in
their lives for a fair length of time, and that they should handle,
therefore, any sexual tensions with them in ways that protect the
relationship. As girls they had been socialized to avoid conflict
and to try to please others. As adult women, this concern with
not hurting others becomes almost a *moral* imperative.[18] The closer
the friendship and work ties, the more women feel responsible
for keeping the relationship on good terms, which may mean ignor-
ing or overlooking discordant messages, and taking the blame for
any misunderstandings.

In direct contrast to the feeling of responsibility that women have in relationships with friends and co-workers, men who are met by accident and who can be cast into the role of "casuals" provide a kind of relief from that female ethic. The woman is not responsible for their relationship, because "there isn't one." She has a great deal of control and freedom. She can simply treat him as a one-night stand:

We met in the hospital waiting room and went out to dinner and had a real nice talk. Real good. I probably shouldn't have gone out with him alone but it seemed he would be disappointed and he seemed very nice. After dinner, I invited him up for a drink.

I just sort of invited him—no, I provoked him into making a pass. We were sitting on the davenport talking and I remember leaning forward to rub my back because it was aching, and that was a very provocative thing to do, and he reached over to rub it, too, and then he just sort of grabbed. I just sort of gave it up and asked him to spend the night. So he did. It wasn't deliberate—conscious—but I take full responsibility.

Brief encounters are seen as essentially "safe" because the man frequently lives in another city; because they have not met "properly"; because flirtations are harmless; and because the woman can shed her moral imperative of having to care about the other's feelings more than her own. Since it is increasingly legitimate for women to have one-night stands, if they so choose, they can define the sexual encounter as essentially a meaningless lark or a release from responsibility. Because this new way of defining sex has become more acceptable, moreover, a sexual experience with even an old friend or work mate can be rationalized and defused by defining it as a "one-night stand," a temporary aberration that does not alter the original basis of the relationship. This process is illustrated by the young executive who was routinely meeting her boss at the disco for "business":

One night we went out and either I was vulnerable or I don't know what, but he ended up coming back to my place. He didn't stay overnight but called me the next morning. It was like, "Are you okay?" The perfect gentleman. And we talked at length about how this might affect work and I said, if anything, let's just call it a fluke. We were both a little looped. I'm not a one-night stand kind of person, but I felt pretty good about saying that's what happened, because the job was what mattered.

If work or friendship is what really matters, casting him into the temporary role of a one-night stand lets the woman hold onto her original definition of the situation. It allows her to return the relationship back to "normal."

Casting the married man in her life into a familiar, safe role of friend, workmate or casual, though, has some unanticipated consequences: While the single woman continues to think of the married man as being in a safe role, her attraction to him can grow free of guilt or undue expectations. The familiar role conceals the undercurrent. She can explain to herself why they are together: he is her friend, boss, mentor, or just another in the series. She can convince herself that "nothing unusual is going on."[19] The lengths to which some women go in refusing to recognize that the potential relationship has become kinetic is noteworthy. One woman invited the married man to stay at her apartment while he was "on the road," but was convinced she had invited him as she would any friend, and only as a friend. Another disavowed any ulterior motive was operative, other than friendship, when her male friend brought a bottle of champagne to her house late one evening. Another justified her boss's nightly phone calls as only attentiveness to her career. Another believed her supervisor's car really did break down, forcing them to spend the night in a motel. His request for a single room—but with two beds—she was certain was based only on economic considerations.

Refusing to recognize what is actually going on, at this point, protects her from potential hurt: If he does not care about me except as a friend/boss/mentor/colleague/casual, then he cannot reject me. It protects her feelings of self-esteem: If he values me for my person or my work skills, then I am not only worthy but I am not a potential deviant, an "other woman" in the making. It protects her from putting her eggs in broken baskets: If he is not going to be interested in me, I will not have to invest in him. It protects her from being steered off her main course: If he is not my lover, he has no say over my choices in life, my agendas. The list of self-reassurances could probably go on indefinitely, with each woman having a set of particular needs that denial fulfills. In this respect, she is probably quite similar to "regular" women: Denial is one of the primary mechanisms all women have for adapting to and surviving in a male-dominated world. Although denial may work for the individual woman, however, it perpetuates the conditions which required the denial in the first place because she does not try to change them. She does not acknowledge how those conditions are shaping her life.

After all of this is said, though, it would be naive and misleading to argue that no single women are out looking for married men. Some are open to the possibility:

> I realized that when he asked me out to dinner that this was certainly not going to be on a business level. This was after my divorce was final, and I guess I was sort of in a "what the hell" kind of experimental mood. I thought, if he's willing to do it, I'll do it too. Just like you read in a book, right?

Others purposefully seek liaisons with married men. Some are women who have "careers" as the Other Woman, and who define themselves as "mistresses." One attractive woman said her career "strategy" was to "trade up"; to use each lover as a "steppingstone." Meeting each new lover through her previous one, she had "moved up" from a lawyer to a judge to a senator; she planned to enter the "world of finance" next. Another woman purposefully sought out married men and expected to be treated like a "mistress in a movie":

I don't date single men. I've got my principles! With married men, I get all the goodies without the hassles. I get a relationship in which I can feel special to someone without having to make a commitment to him. Usually, when you got a guy who is married you got a runner. He's a sleep-around or he wouldn't be sleeping around to begin with. It's kind of fun to pull him out of the chase and see how long you can keep him. The competition is not with the wife, but with the other "other women." Plural. And it's fun to play that game.

These self-defined mistresses, though, are not typical of the majority of contemporary Other Women who have repeated relationships with married men. The majority are women who have not planned on being involved with married men; they do not call themselves "mistresses," and they do not make their living that way. Rather, they happen into their first relationship, and their second, and perhaps their third, much in the same way as most Other Women do—by accident, unintentionally. What happens, though, is that through their experiences as an Other Woman they come to value that kind of relationship. Having experienced such a relationship, they become skilled in recognizing cues from married men and in giving cues that will not be misinterpreted.

There are two groups of women with poor probabilities of finding single men to date: middle-aged and older divorcees and young professional women. Women in these categories are likely to have serial relationships with married men, although for different reasons. A 50-year-old, divorced dance instructor illustrates the role of married *men* in a middle-aged woman's life:

I don't look for married men, exactly—believe me, I wish I could find some single men to date. But the ones out there are low in quality and I don't like singles' bars. I'm 50 years old. The choice is not to date, or to date married men. I meet them through my life. On vacation. At my son's commissioning ceremony. Where I work. All the interesting ones are married.

As women age, the pool of available, interesting single men becomes smaller and smaller, and singles' activities favor the younger woman. To ask a woman of 50 or more to compete in a singles bar, for example, is cruel and unusual. A woman in her middle years, then, should she desire male companions, may find them only among the married. Compounding the problem of the increasing numbers of middle-aged divorced women is their limited incomes. Many have depended upon their husbands economically, and are working in low-paying jobs. They may come to appreciate in a utilitarian way the extras a man can provide—dinners, rose bushes, trips, clothing. Better to have a married man who will provide some of the amenities of life, than no man at all. For the dance instructor, and others like her, involvement with a married man is an integral part of an economic survival strategy. In her case, there is a coterie of married men, none of whom knows about the others, from whom she expects to receive gifts and courtly manners. Moreover, she is ambivalent about getting married:

I don't want to get married just to be getting married. I frankly don't want a lot of the crap that goes with marriage. I'm very ambivalent about this.

In direct contrast to her, is a never-married government attorney in her mid-thirties. In the past eight years, she has had four relationships with married men and is on the threshold of a fifth. The first four men were colleagues; the "new one" she met on a canoe trip. At this point in her life, she prefers married men:

I like having my independence. Not being smothered. What's right for me is not a lot of heavy emotional stuff. I'm not sure you can pull this off with a single man. I'm not sure that I'd have as much control. It scares the shit out of me to lose control. I was really done in once by a man very badly.
    The best relationship I've ever had was with a married man. It was not a love romantic relationship at all, but for

me it was really right. He was a black man and was like
every Jewish girl's dream. Gorgeous body. The ultimate forbidden. I didn't get smothered. It was playful. And the sex
was like fireworks.

In many ways, she epitomizes that class of women who have
grown up with an undersupply of men and who have come of
age during the women's and sexual liberation movements. As is
true of many women of her generation, she has been hurt by a
single man, and she wants to avoid having that experience repeated.
Due to the new cultural ideologies and opportunities for women,
she can, in fact, lead a fairly autonomous, economically independent life. And because of the liberation movements of the seventies,
she can reduce the importance of a man in her life to his sexual
abilities:

Why bother being with a man unless the sex is good? There
is no other point. Women are nicer people. They're better
friends, more loyal, warmer, and they have much more empathy than men. So the only point in having a relationship
with a man is good sex. If you don't have that, why bother?

Unlike the middle-aged dance instructor, this woman does not
need or want a man to "take care" of her financially or emotionally.
She does not need a man to provide manly courtesies, only "good
sex." She genuinely values women. And, unlike the dance instructor, this attorney does not equivocate about marriage:

I don't want to get married. I like living alone. I like having
control of my own finances. The things that marriage is
supposed to give you are not sure things. Many of my married friends don't even have companionship. My friends provide me with a social life, and I have my own little bundle
of money. All I want now is some good sex.

For the most part, experienced Other Women are able to keep
their relationships with married men "cool." They are able to keep

some distance and control, for they have experienced more of these relationships, and have developed strategies for protecting themselves, emotionally. They are adept at casting the married man into the role of "another married man." But even they sometimes misjudge what is going on and lose control—indeed that is what has happened to both the middle-aged dance instructor and the younger attorney. Both of them, to their surprise, have become emotionally involved with married men.

But that this happens to both the experienced and the novitiate, should really be no surprise: The way the social world is currently constructed, liaisons between married men and single women are likely to abound. Demographically, there are many more single women who have increased mobility at work and at play, and who increasingly enter previously all-male preserves. The sheer number of interactions augments the probability of some of them escalating. Many single women are in a state of personal change, moving into new roles and holding transitory positions, making them open to new experiences. Encounters between males and females continue to have sexual overtones, with men defining the situation differently—as more sexual—than women. Because women continue to believe that men are "just" friends, mentors, or colleagues, they ignore the cues that signal to themselves, and the married man, that the emotional level is escalating.

Because the number of potential relationships is so great, it is predictable that some of them will deepen. During this early "getting involved" phase of the relationship, time is spent together, and time is spent thinking about the relationship. The woman begins really to like this man; even women who are normally somewhat cool and distant in relationships describe their relations with a married man as good and comfortable, intriguing, valuable, and exciting, and the man as good, kind, intelligent, interesting, and so on. At this point in the relationship with a married man, "innocence is bliss."

Chapter Three

HAVING SEX

Relationships between single women and married men are commonly thought of and talked about as sexual relationships; having sex is the presumed raison d'être. Heterosexual norms are so strong, the social-scientific research so narrow, and the common wisdom so entrenched, that this belief must be considered briefly before discussing the role that sex actually does play in contemporary relationships between married men and single women.

Until quite recently, research on extramarital relationships has viewed them as though the sexual component were their primary or only component.[1] Moreover, the research has focused almost entirely on the married man's sexual needs and experiences, rather than on the single woman's. In sum, the kind of social-scientific research that has been done reflects general cultural beliefs about sex and sexuality and not necessarily the actual experiences of men and women involved extramaritally.

One of the most central of those beliefs is that sex is the province of men, and as such it can be "had," "accomplished," "achieved." Men come to women for sex, and they have "it" with them. The language we use to talk about sex objectifies and masculinizes it. Men are seen as needing and wanting "it" more than women do. Some researchers have proposed that that cultural idea reflects a male's biological needs. Adultery, they argue, is based on "man's [male's] animal inheritance, and may be attributable to identifiable nervous system properties."[2] When the nervous system gets the same stimulation over and over again, arousal is sluggish. After a while, for example, male chimpanzees are more smitten with bowling balls and wire female chimpanzee dolls than with their mates. Psychological fatigue, the researchers contend, is the reason men—like chimpanzees—wander: monogamy is "too" exhausting for the nervous system.

Many purveyors of marital advice contend that sex is of *overwhelming* importance to men. For example, Marabel Morgan, author of *The Total Woman,* asserts that husbands turn to "other women" for sexual renewal. In order for a wife to prevent this, she should be like an "angel of sex," resurrecting her husband's interest in her.[3] Lois Bird, author of *How to Be a Happily Married Mistress,* asks wives, "Would he pick you for his mistress? A mistress seduces. A wife submits." Routinely, professional and familial advice givers assert that the way to a man's heart, and to keeping his heart, is through his genitals.[4]

Sex, then, becomes something that men want but women control.[5] "It" is a battleground where women supposedly have greater power because they can use their sexuality to manipulate men. Women are divided thereby into two categories: wives, who manipulate their husbands by withholding sex, and mistresses, who manipulate them by proferring it.[6] Men are stereotyped, too, as bestial creatures, subdued by sexual good times, and the errant husband as a rapacious adolescent boy, out of control.

Although there is little doubt that males are socialized to place greater importance on "having" sex than women are, to label relationships between married men and single women as solely or primarily about sex androcentrizes, distorts, and falsifies them. Worse, the normative blinders prevent us from seeing what part sex actually does play in these relationships. Just as women's sexuality, generally, has been ignored until quite recently, so have the sexual life and experiences of the Other Woman: We know virtually nothing about them.

Other Women are first and foremost *women,* and as such they have much in common with all women, including attitudes toward sexuality. Like most women, they have been socialized to be sexually repressed. The sexual repression of women, along with the sexual double standard, probably originated in the desire of men to ensure that their biological offspring would inherit their property. Although sexual expectations for women are changing, the sexually inhibiting socialization persists because women who are sexually repressed raise daughters in their own image; they train them by word and deed to minimize the importance of their own sexual needs and preferences.[7] Women involved with married men have had the same socialization and share the same attitudes. They are likely to downplay the importance of sex for themselves, which is not surprising given the strong cultural message that sex is the domain of men:

> I have a whole lot of problems with sex. I'm almost totally anorgasmic. It was important to me only as another opportunity to please.

> For me, a huge part of our relationship centered around eating. That seemed to be the big thing, to have lunch or dinner somewhere—not sex.

More surprisingly, many Other Women believe that sex is not very important to their married lovers either:

> It's not the sexual aspect that keeps us together. It's the talking, just being together. He's as happy meeting for a half hour or so just to sit and talk.

> As a matter of fact, I couldn't even lure him into bed lots of times. It wasn't his shot. Whatever he wanted from me, that wasn't it.

> Because of his age, he was rarely able to get much of an erection. I don't know whether a 65-year-old man can, but he couldn't get much of one. There was never much inter-

course because he couldn't do anything. So he used to just like to lay in bed naked or he loved to take baths together, that kind of thing.

Because women and men have different perspectives on sexuality, the Other Women may not be totally correct in their assessments of their lovers' interests. As women, they will tend to downplay the sexual element of their relationship more so than men would. But, even so, it seems clear that a great deal more than sex is going on between the couple: talking, eating, or just being together. Time is spent in other activities besides sex, and it is these that the Other Woman, at least, sees as more relevant.

Perpetuating the idea that these relationships are primarily sexual, however, diminishes the stature of the Other Woman. Wives can think of her as the husband's "sex object," a nonperson. The Other Women is stigmatized and depersonalized. Thinking of her one-dimensionally may help the wife cope with her husband's infidelity, but her coping profits the man more than either of the women: she can become a "total woman," devoting her life to him; she can forgive him because his transgression is of the body, not of the mind or soul; she can blame the Other Woman for using her sexual wiles to entrap her husband, thereby displacing anger away from him; she can fight for him, thereby enlarging his ego.

Defining these relationships as primarily sexual, even if they are not, though, affords men a culturally legitimated rationalization for extramarital liaisons. Between their biological "needs" and merciless women preying upon those needs, they are not fallen husbands, but manipulated gonads.

Although the cultural stereotypes may justify a man's extramarital relationship, they do not explain it. That there is such an elaborate rationalization for the *male's* violation of his marriage vows, but virtually no cultural rationalization for the single woman's transgression, testifies to the severe disjunction in sexual norms governing male and female behavior. It is to those norms and our sexual socialization that we must look in order to understand how sex is brought into relationships between single women and married men, and the role it plays in those relationships.

In our society, sexuality is distinctly different from any other behavior in that moral imperatives are intertwined with conscious and unconscious fantasies. On the one hand, the pleasurable, sensual feelings aroused through sexual contact are hard to dispel as morally wrong, and on the other one's actual sexual experiences may fall short of the fantasized ones. Since sexual socialization begins in the crib where infants are restrained from exploring their bodies and continues in the playyard where toddlers are reprimanded for exploring each other's bodies, the feelings many adults have about sex as "bad" are deeply embedded and primitive. Ambivalent and deeply seated feelings about sex are brought into adult sexual relationships, which make them personally risky: one's fantasy might not be met; one can be rejected; one can be disappointed; one might get punished—be found out, get pregnant, be abused, or be mortified.

Today, those old risks are compounded because even greater normative confusion exists; the old rules governing sex were repressive, whereas the new ones are permissive. It is hard to "read" the other, hard to read yourself, and even harder to know if the other reads you as you think you want to be read. If this were not true, how else would we explain the plethora of movies, novels, songs, poems, and soap operas devoted to the theme of "Does s/he or doesn't s/he want me?"

But, if the realm of acceptable sexuality is normatively murky, sex in culturally disapproved liaisons, such as adulterous ones, is virtually a quagmire. The undergrowth of cultural ambiguity and personal ambivalence reaches the surface, entangled. Whenever a sexually deviant relationship is being considered, a great deal of vacillation occurs because the personal risks are much greater than those in approved sexual exchanges. There is much more to lose. The other party may label you a deviant, talk to others about your perversion and gall, or ridicule you.[8] Or, you may lose your job, your spouse, or your reputation.

One of the ways to destigmatize a deviant sexual relationship is to *normalize it in all other respects.* [9] So, for example, since the "chase" is still a major feature of regular, normal heterosexuality, the married man who is direct and persistent in his sexual request is acting like a *normal* man, not a sex maniac or a deviant. Even if the woman resists, he can interpret the fact that she continues to see him as "yes, eventually," for that would be the *normal* meaning of her behavior. He can persist with impunity:

> It was six months before I had any sexual relationship with him. I resisted sex, and then finally I gave in. It was one of those things when you are finally tired and it just clicked. He was there in the hotel and on and on and on so I finally gave in.

> He really laid it on me that weekend that he wanted to go to bed with me and stuff. We were walking on the beach and for the 85th time that weekend he raised it.

Despite the many changes in sexual norms in society, men are still likely to initiate sexual intercourse.[10] Although women have much more sexual freedom today, it is not yet considered normal for a woman actively and persistently to pursue a man sexually, and most women still are not comfortable initiating sex.[11] Ironically, even a "sexually liberated woman" may have to dredge up the old, unliberated seduction rituals because of males' resistance to "pushy" women. A single woman desiring sex with a reluctant married man may have to provide a sexually suggestive and sexually opportune setting:

> He was 57, a lovely person, who had not been around very much. We'd been negotiating the relationship in the mails for about nine months. He was very clumsy about it. When he came into town, I smoothed the way. Suggested where to have dinner, very romantic place. Then, I said, "Let's go to my house for a while." I set it up. Not pushing him into it, but setting it up. He didn't know it was really going to be sexual.

Acting in sexually traditional ways—being persistent if a male, seductive if a female—then, can contribute to transforming the relationship into a sexual one. But so can simply acting in socially traditional ways. Just by following the norms that govern male and female *sociability,* sexuality can become a possibility. This is so because the norms empower men and help them, should they choose, to transform a platonic relationship into a sexually active one. For example, men have the right to invade the personal space of women.[12] Men can phone women, invite themselves over, touch their bodies. Accepting these overtures is tantamount to "asking for it":

He had been asking me to have a drink with him for some time. This time I decided what the hell. I can remember him touching my hand, arm around, hand-holding, that sort of stuff. Once that starts to happen, you either pull away or say what the hell.

"Coach" had great legs. All the girls at the gym were chasing him. He started to phone me to talk about my workout schedule. Eventually, he said he wanted to share a bottle of sherry with me. So he trotted over to my house and opened up the sherry. He decided to show me his legs, and that's how it got started. He wore little bikinis. One thing led to another and the next thing you know we were in bed. It finally hit me that he was really interested in me. My whole perception of him and the relationship changed. I thought he was exceedingly attractive. I thought how could he possibly be interested in me.

Not only has "Coach" taken the male privilege of phoning and coming over, he has also used a classic ploy: let the alcohol do the rubbing. Not seeing herself as attractive enough, she thinks she cannot compete with the other women clamoring for him. Not until they are making love does it "hit" her that he finds her attractive and that sex was on his agenda. Being perceived as "a catch" helps a man transform a platonic relationship into a sexual one because women feel flattered by the attention of such a man; women have been socialized to please; women have been taught to believe that if they best out other women in the hot game of catch-him-if-you-can, they are worthwhile. These are all rules of regular male-female interactions that continue to be operative despite the new changes. They are rules favoring males.

Although women may strive to escape these norms, this is impossible because the rules favoring males in sexual and nonsexual relationships with women are deeply entrenched, omnipresent, and not always recognized as giving men an advantage. For example, one of the primary ways in which males exert an advantage over women is through their less self-demanding definitions of friendship. Not only is a woman's definition of friendship more intimate and involving, as has been discussed earlier, but her definition also makes her less powerful in her relationships with men, because as a friend she expects herself to be agreeable, sympathetic, and forgiving. Men consider friendship as buddyship; hanging out together. Her definition makes her self-sacrificing to the demands of friendship, and emotionally vulnerable to her friends. Most telling, men separate friendship with a woman from sex and love.[13] Relationships between single women and married men are frequently defined as friendships by the single women; indeed, even mentoring and collegial relationships are often overlaid with feelings of friendship. Because friendship is a necessary preamble to sex for many women, it is not surprising that sex eventually follows:

> Friends turn into lovers and that was what happened. We did. When I look back on it, I guess I was kidding myself that we might just be friends because I was obviously attracted to him. Why would I be going out with a married man I wasn't even remotely attracted to? Obviously there was something there and I was willing to chance a friendship because I enjoyed him and thought I could keep things in control. I am still amazed he held on as long as he did, because there was nothing sexual about it.

Cultural ambiguity and personal ambivalence about sex can lead to misinterpretation, norms supporting male privilege and power give men the right to initiate, escalate, and transform relationships, and the foreplay of friendship prepares the woman for a sexual liaison. As in a marriage, once sex occurs, it is usually there for the duration of their relationship, regardless of whether or not the single woman is satisfied with their sex life. The old norm and legal precedent giving a man continuing rights to a woman he has once slept with have not disappeared, even outside marriage.[14]

For some Other Women, as for some wives, the sexual component is an important and satisfying part of her relationship:

> The quality of the sex was superb. We could get together once or twice during the week for three or four hours to screw in a variety of ways. It was really marvelous—so much so that once or twice a week really was enough. We really couldn't handle much more than that.

But for some Other Women, like for some wives, sex lacks emotional intimacy or is not physically satisfying:

> Because the relationship was long-distance, it was always like running off and having a two-week affair. There was never anything dreary or old fashioned about it, because we never had time to get bored with it. It was passionate sex, but it was lacking emotional intimacy. Ultimately, it was not a good sex life.

> We were close, but I think we went to bed a total of three times. His thing was to talk about it a lot. He thought he was just marvelous. I used to do the vibrator before we got together because I knew he was so bad.

Other Women, then, like wives, appraise their sex lives differently. Unlike earlier generations, contemporary women have access to knowledge about sexuality upon which to base their evaluations. Many have slept with more than one man: they have sexual experiences and sexual expectations, giving them data to compare and contrast. Research on women's orgasmic possibilities and sexual fantasies is widely available. Women can talk to each other about their sexuality and share their knowledge. What has not changed, though, is women's apparent willingness, despite their knowledge, expectations, and experiences, to accept a less than satisfying sexual relationship.

Traditional wives have had much to gain by sexual compliance, but why would a contemporary single woman accept a nonsatisfying sexual relationship with a married man? Part of the answer rests in the demographic issues discussed earlier—many women think any man is better than none—and part rests in her acceptance of the normative definitions of women's sexuality as unimportant. But, we can answer that question more directly and at the same time understand the sex life of the single woman more clearly by posing a different question: What purposes does having sex with a married man fulfill? Why have sex with a married man?

Sex with a married man permits a single woman to explore her sexuality and to redefine her sexual self with greater freedom and control than she has when sexually involved with a single man. Although a contemporary woman claims the right to define her own sexuality, she often enough finds that a dating relationship with an emphasis on the future stifles her sexual freedom and exploration. She sabotages herself. But, in a relationship with a married man, because it is outside the bonds of convention she can *experiment* and *practice* new definitions of her sexual self. Such a relationship gives her both time and freedom to redefine herself.

Sexual repression has been a major factor in the socialization and social control of women. The images of the "virgin" and the "whore," Mary and Eve pervade the culture. Men, women are told, may sleep with "whores" but they seek "good women" as wives. Cautionary tales abound. Little, though, has been said about women's attraction to upstanding men as husbands and ne'er-do-wells as lovers. Judging from the recent spate of movies with this theme, its resonance in women's consciousness is greater than the discussion about it: A socially deviant relationship is a way for women to overcome their sexual repression.

By having a sexual relationship with a married man, the woman violates moral, religious, and social strictures. She is an adulterer.

Once she has violated social and religious conventionality, the possibility of suspending other sexually restrictive norms also arises.[15] Moreover, because there are no guidelines on how she should "do sex" with a married man, she can distance herself from her own sexual history:

> It was phenomenal. For the first time, I broke out of my family's rigidity. He touched, he held, he cuddled, he foreplayed, he let me feel like I could be a woman. I didn't have to be afraid to do crazy things, not necessarily off-the-wall things, but just things that I knew in my Protestant-ethic family probably had never been broached. I learned I could wear sexy nightgowns and be sexy. And I could be sexually aggressive which I had *never* thought in my life I would do.

Nothing in her previous sexual history had given this woman, and others like her, license to "let go." Relationships with married lovers do because they are dissociated from the family and community, and from the investment and future orientation of a marital relationship. "Brazen" women can feel good about themselves.

Because the sexual inhibition of women has had such a long history, it takes many different forms. One form is a woman's willful desexualization of herself through weight gain, poor fitting clothes, stooped posture, and so on. It is as though women believe that if they make themselves sexually unattractive, their sexual problems will disappear. For an overweight woman whose mother had told her she was ugly, unwanted, unlovable, and boring, even to her therapist, a relationship with a married man helped her overcome her sexual fears:

> My weight problem was a way of defending myself against being a sexual person. I had been overweight my entire life and have felt tremendously insecure about my sexuality. Food was partly a substitute for sex, and my weight kept me out of circulation—or had me believe that I was out of

circulation. My weight didn't matter to him and I found I could let go with him because I knew it wasn't going to go anywhere.

Although nearly all women have been sexually inhibited, some have been so suppressed that a radical split with their background is necessary, if they are to have an active sexual life. One woman, a schoolteacher, whose mother told her sex was evil and degrading and any enjoyment of it would be punished, and who had been married to a man whose mother had washed out his mouth with soap and locked him in the cellar when he asked her what was meant by the immaculate conception, carried a picture of her married lover, a full-length profile shot of a nude black man, fully erect. He was a blue-collar worker, an uncle of one of her students. She said:

He is the only man I've been able to touch. He has an all night hard. Total control. He's sensual, never bumbling. The really amazing thing was that I didn't carry any of the baggage from my upbringing and my marriage into the relationship. With my husband, I had never reached climax. His idea of sex was to do it as infrequently as possible and for as short as possible. Five minutes from first kiss to completion, maybe once a month. With him [married lover], I could come six times a night. He kisses me and I come.

For this woman, whose sexuality had been nearly eliminated, the multiple forbiddens of her lover's race, lower occupational status, uncle status to one of her students, and marital status allowed her to break through her own sexual biography. In this respect, she is similar to many women: By having sex with an "inappropriate" man, by tasting the "forbidden fruit," she can experience her own sexuality. Because the forbidden is supposed to arouse us sexually, indeed, that is a good part of why it is forbidden, tabooed encounters are experienced as sexually exciting.

Sex with a married man gives women a chance to escape some

old tyrannies. They can feel greater freedom because being with a married man suspends the rules of propriety. Without a future orientation or normative dating expectations, they can give themselves time and space to undo sexual inhibitions. By reducing their inhibitions, they begin to feel sexually empowered, rather than passive victims or objects, which, in turn, raises their self-esteem; an enhanced sense of self-worth may lead to even greater feelings of sexual empowerment.[16]

In addition to dealing with old repressions, sexuality with a married man allows women to deal with the new permissiveness: It permits them to embrace a definition of themselves as sexual abstainers *for the time being.* Because the man is married, a woman can legitimately say no. Not much explanation is necessary on her part; a simple, "But, you're married," suffices. She may want affection but not a sexual relationship, as was the case with a woman trying to establish a career and lay to rest a painful divorce. Because her history had been one of "sexual slavery to her own body," through which she "frittered away her time and lost herself," she welcomed a "sexually minimal," long-distance relationship with a married man.

For many women today, having sex creates problems. Although they think they *should* be able to dissociate sex from stronger emotions, they are not able to do so. Many find that once sex is brought into their relationships they are disempowered, and their identity and independence is threatened. Not having the experience or tools to counter their socialization, they lose control, not just over their bodies, but over other parts of their lives, because they adapt themselves to the man's needs and preferences:

I have a hard time separating sex and love. If I had sex with a man then I ended up being in love with him. This body thing I don't understand, and I don't think men have it. I didn't want to be in love, but I wanted a man's attentions. I could put off sex because he was married.

Whenever I had sex with a man, I found I succumbed to his definitions of who and what I should be—not just sexually, but in all sorts of ways. I needed a period of sexual celibacy, but not total withdrawal from all affection, in order to be able to define myself. To find out what it was I wanted to do with my life. Not what some man thought was good for me. He understood, and didn't press me.

In earlier eras, virginity and abstinence were expectations for single women. Our unmarried foremothers were not required to defend a celibate existence; nor did they have to exclude single men from their dating lives because of the overbearing sexual demands of those men. But celibacy today as a *chosen* way of life goes against the sexual liberation ideology; women in dating relationships have to justify no sex. Although the new sexual freedom for women should include the right to abstain, single women perceive single men as not respecting that right:

Single guys think you owe them sex because they're so nice to go out with you. Yuck. There's this whole thing with this men shortage or something and single men think they're just so swell to date you. The pits.

Relationships with married men, then, allow heterosexual women to explore their sexuality in two seemingly contradictory ways: it allows them to say yes when they have been previously reticent to do so; and it allows them to say no without a brass band backing them up. Both responses afford women the chance to define and take control over their own sexual activities; to wrest from men the power to define them, sexually. Similarly, these relationships give women space to explore their sexual orientations. One woman, who was unsure of her sexual preference, even though she was involved with another woman, found that having a sexual relationship with a married man did not threaten her woman lover the way a relationship with a single man had. Her female lover saw the married man relationship as trivial and temporary. Another woman who was uncertain as to whether she was a lesbian said:

Because he was married, I didn't have to sleep with him a lot, but it was important to me to sleep with him because it was one of the ways I concealed to myself that I was a lesbian. I could say to myself I was still sleeping with men. He could never stay overnight about which I was glad because I didn't have to go through that morning thing. Single men were too much like they owned me. Like since they slept with me once they had the right to do it whenever they wanted and you had no right to say no.

Eventually, this woman, who genuinely enjoyed the caressing and fondling aspects of her relationship, found sexual intercourse so unpleasant, and the life that heterosexual women were expected to lead so repellent, that she came out as a lesbian. Her relationship with a married man permitted her to explore at her own pace and with limited psychological struggle her heterosexuality. Single men had not given her that option.

For women who know they are lesbians, but who are closeted, a relationship with a married man can serve as a cover:

> For lesbians, married men are great because you don't have to fuck them too much. When you need to be with a man or have your co-workers believe you are, you can use them. Gay men used to be good for that but too many people nowadays know when a guy is gay. Out-of-town married men are the greatest.

Lesbian women, then, find they can limit their sexual exchanges with married men more easily than with single men; they can use their relationships to discover their sexual orientation, or to keep it a secret.

For both lesbian and heterosexual women, sex with a married man is less demanding and less potentially oppressive than sex with a single man because the woman claims the rights she tends to relinquish in regular male-female relationships. She claims the right to sexual freedom; the right to abstain without derision; and the right to opt out of heterosexuality all together. None of these rights are as available to her in *practice* in a regular relationship because those relationships are tied to larger, more entrenched, familial and community expectations.

Although sex with a married man gives a single woman the opportunity and time to find herself sexually, there is another, more traditional use of sex, namely, the exchange of sexual favors for economic rewards. In place of the occasional courtesan of the past has entered a large number of ordinary, everyday women who are in need of money: they are going back to school; they are divorced and raising children; they hold low-paying jobs. Unlike storybook mistresses, most real Other Women do not plan to exchange sex for money. One divorced woman who was about to enter graduate school in another state, and whose relationship with a married man had been platonic, explained how he became her "sugar daddy":

He took me to his home, which was huge. It looked like a funeral home, very ugly. He said he wanted me to see where he lived. He handed me a check for $500, to help me out in school. I handed it back and said, "No, I don't need the money."

After that, we went out some more to real expensive restaurants. I made it real clear that I didn't want any sexual involvement, particularly after the money offer. I wasn't going to be a prostitute. He went on and on how that wasn't his intention. That he just wanted to help me out. He insisted there were no strings attached, and I finally did take the check.

After she started graduate school, he sent her a "couple hundred dollars a month," bought some furniture, and paid off the $3500 still owed on her car. He came to see her fairly often:

I was in the hotel with him—I think it was the weekend he laid out about $1000 for rugs for me—and I finally just said okay [to having sex]. I never enjoyed sex with him. I kept always feeling guilty about it because he was helping me out financially. There was a little bit of this kind of prostitute thing that I was giving this sex in return for financial help.

I don't regret having done it. The whole experience of having had a sugar daddy adds a dimension to me, another part. It was a learning experience. I was able to take material things without giving much back. I couldn't have done that with a single man. The financial benefits at the time were very nice and very helpful.

Although some women accidentally "happen into" a financial arrangement, others seek out married men of some means to provide "the niceties" that they cannot afford themselves. For example, the middle-aged dance instructor, discussed earlier, depends upon her married "boyfriends" to augment her meager income by taking her out to dinner, on trips, and by providing presents for the house. Holding traditional attitudes towards men's financial responsibilities toward women, she expects them to provide for her.

Neither the student nor the dance instructor, nor the Other Women like them, are prostitutes, although they exchange sexual favors for economic ones; in that, of course, they are not very different from many dates or many wives. The student and the dance instructor, living on small incomes, depend upon the economic benefits that men can provide. Because single women are frequently at poverty or near poverty levels, married men as an economic resource cannot be discounted; having sex with a married man can become an integral part of their economic survival strategy. Since economic equality between the sexes is not likely in the near future, some single women will continue to depend upon married men for economic advantages that their own work does not provide.

From the perspective of most single women, sex is not the primary reason for their relationship with a married man—nor do they think that sex is his primary motive, either. And although their sex life may be neutral or negative, sex with a married man has some secondary benefits: it allows them to explore their sexuality at their own pace; to work out sexual repression or to limit sexual occasions; it gives them an opportunity to explore their sexual orientation; and they may exchange it for economic benefits.

Regardless, though, of the secondary uses sex has within the relationship, because women are women, sex carries many cultural messages that increase the emotional cost of their relationships. Although sex can be discussed as though it were separable from one's emotions, most women do not experience it that way. It is hard for them to consider sex as "just" sex. Because many women believe that if you are friends and then have sex, love must be what you feel—or that if the sex is good, it must be love, many of them, unbeknown to themselves, and despite their belief that they are in control, are teetering on the brink of love. Some are going to fall. Hard.

Chapter Four

COULD THIS BE
LOVE?

AH, LOVE. We say that love comes like a "bolt out of the blue."
It just happens. It hits like the flu, leaving one weak, out of control,
no longer quite oneself. But, in fact, love does not just happen
by chance. Although love feels uniquely personal to the individual,
the feeling we label love is socially generated, socially prescribed,
and socially learned. Even our reluctance to demystify it is socially
given. Thinking about love as something we have no control over
justifies behavior we would not normally condone. In the name
of love, we are "swept away."[1]

In medieval times, love potions and charms, aphrodisiacs and
philtres were sold by cunning sorts to provoke an unlawful love,
a love that crossed the stars, or classes, or familial bounds. The
purveyors of the potions could be sentenced to death, so important
and yet so susceptible to magic the course of love was thought
to be by our philosophical and social ancestors.[2]

If the perpetrators of "unlawful love" between single women
and married men were to be eradicated today, the conditions of
modern life, themselves, would have to be dismantled. They are
the love potions, the aphrodisiacs. The way our world is organized,
single women are going to fall in love, often and unintentionally,
with married men.

For women of earlier generations, women with few options other than marriage, falling in love with a man who could economically provide for them, a man who would be a dutiful husband and good father, was desirable. Economic dependency dictated to a great measure the men one fell in love with.[3] For contemporary women, although financial dependency still plays a major role in a marriage choice, *being in love* has some new meanings. Love is associated with the freedom to be oneself, with emotional intimacy, with feeling good about oneself, and with a feeling of belonging to another.[4] Love is being free *and* safe, independent *and* close. These feelings, as we shall see, are the ones likely to be generated in a relationship with a married man.

Single women describe their married lovers as "ideal," "every woman's dream," "compassionate and exciting," "like no man ever known before." Even women who are later embittered see their married lovers as "very special," "unique." Like a Greek chorus, women chant over and over again the Olympian virtues of their married lovers:

He was everything any woman could want in a man.

Everyone, men and women, loved him. It's not fair to compare other men to him, because no one is ever going to be like him.

He was a creative genius.

And they chant over and over again the splendor of their love:

I was absolutely in love with him and I have never felt and never expect to feel again as in love with anyone again, and I have never been.

I'm just overwhelmed. Stunned. I've only admitted to being in love once before.

He taught me how to love somebody, and this was perfect love.

Despite one's inclination to dismiss these praises of the lover and relationship as pure romanticism and rationalization, the theme is so persistent, present even in those women who prefer emotionally distant relationships, that it cannot be denied and should not be minimized: Single women are not only finding married men "nice," "interesting," and "fun," many are falling in love with them.

One of the reasons that women fall in love in these relationships is that some old ideas about love are brought into the relationship. One of these is the idea that falling in love is a natural, almost inevitable, outgrowth of friendship:

> I told him it was not going to be a sexual relationship, and if he didn't like it that way, fine. I put him on hold. I put him on hold for so long to see if he really cared about me as a person. The time gave me a sense of security. He likes me for me. I'm not just another affair. When I finally realized that I really cared about him, it was almost too late not to be in love with him.

> He was the first man I had ever been involved with that we were friends first. Just friends, and there was just the closeness of just being good friends. And I guess the closeness just developed into love.

Passivity and the "giving into" quality that has characterized women's relationships with men persist. If he proves he really cares by acting like a friend, not demanding sex, she can hardly help herself if she ends up really caring for him. Similarly, because for many women sex is still tied to love, should their sexual relationship feel like a union of body and emotions, she is likely to think she is in love:

> I had grown up believing that sex and love went together. When we went to bed, that night, I knew I was in love with him.

All the guys I had slept with had been macho-men. He was so caring. I didn't know sex could be this way. I thought we must be in love because how else could the sex be so special?

Still others, the more traditionally romantic, can pinpoint a particular event, the exemplary occasion, when they knew the relationship had deepened and been transformed into love:

I realized I really cared for him on the Friday before my birthday. He took me out and because I turned 33, he wanted to take me to 33 dives, bars, and just have a good time. He was crazy. Until that night I had always seen him as a serious corporate business type of person. We had a lot of fun. He bought me a T-shirt that said, "Somebody in Cincinnati loves you." And I looked at him and said, "Do you?" That was the major turning point. I saw the other side of him.

And for the increasing coterie of women who have been hurt by men—including by their ex-husbands—and who have become experienced at protecting themselves from emotional closeness, the unexpected attentiveness and concern of their married lover brings them to love's playfield where their armor is rattled:

My life didn't have a lot of history of people giving a damn about me. I was real impressed that this man came along and got real concerned about me. All my life there's never been another person who cared about me like him.

He treats me like a queen. He sent me a dozen red roses. Nobody's ever shown me that kind of appreciation. Nobody. Not even my parents on graduation.

In contrast to these women who do not want emotionally close relationships with men because they have been hurt, there is another group of women who want distance because they have other agendas, such as finishing their education or building careers. Few professional women have had a lot of experience with men who genuinely seem to accept them and their career priorities. Should a married man do so, his value is augmented:

> He was aware of my need to get my research underway. Rather than being another complication in my life, he was a real help. He really was sweet about it—he understood how much my work meant to me.

> He was perfect for a person like me, a person who likes her independence and wants to lead her own life. He is very attentive—I didn't expect that and now I think I really do care for him. It's scary but it's nice. And I hadn't planned on that.

Each of the individual accounts make sense: Women do fall in love following feelings of friendship; women do commingle sex with love; women do love men who love them; women do fall in love with men who are good to them and respect them; and women recognize love through the eyes of their lover. Yet, women are friends with many men they do not fall in love with; they have sex with men they do not fall in love with; they receive the kindness of many men they do not fall in love with; and the unrequited love of the male for the unmoved female is the balladeer's lament. Why, then, do so many single women, despite all the protestations and protections to the contrary, find themselves emotionally involved with married men?

One must ask whether or not the man's marital status, itself, might not be somehow structurally conducive to single women falling in love with them. How might the constraints rooted in his married state contribute to her feelings of being in love rather than preventing those feelings? Why do some women who are well-defended against intimacy find themselves emotionally entangled with their married lovers? The answers rest in how his marital status establishes the parameters of their world, and turns it into a *secret* one. Not only is the existence of that world shrouded, the lovers engage in self-disclosures and create a privately shared history. Their world is one surrounded by and saturated in secrecy. Mystical explanations for her falling in love are unnecessary: The conditions—secrecy, privacy, and time constraints—under which her relationship with a married man is built are aphrodisiacal enough to afford ample explanation.

Georg Simmel noted about 80 years ago that the secret, "the hiding of reality," is one of the major achievements of humankind because it permits "an immense enlargement of the world," the possibility of creating a "second world alongside the manifest world."[5] This world can remain the private island of its secret inhabitants, a Fantasy Island all to themselves.

Relationships between single women and married men provide just such a secret island, an immense opportunity to create a second world, to hide reality. Within that secret world, truths can be suspended; fantasy can be acted out; lies can be told; and deception can be practiced. But most salient of all is that the fact of its existence is withheld from many other significant people—her family, her co-workers, his wife, his family: There is always someone who cannot know. The secret is always kept from someone.

Although the contemporary woman involved with a married man may accept herself in that relationship, she is well aware that the cultural stigma has not abated. She is aware, for example, that if she is building a career, she will be accused of having "slept her way to the top." If she is a feminist, she knows that her friends will question her liaison. If she is trying to rear her children as a single parent, she will fear the effects of her "flagrant mistress" status on them. Few women are in positions where they can say "it really doesn't matter who knows," even though they may personally feel that way. For the regular world, the primary one, is still one in which the double standard reigns: Identical behavior on the part of the male and the female garners different rewards.

Although he is the adulterer, she will be labeled the "husband stealer" and "home wrecker," or the person who traded sexual favors for career advantages. Few women, despite their raised consciousness, can escape these cultural dicta. Even fewer can escape the social consequences of those cultural beliefs. Women do get fired, sent to corporate purdah, and "exposed" in the media for being involved with married men.[6]

It is his marital status, then, which sets the stage for the creation of the second world: the hiding of reality. His marital status leads to the relationship being carried on in private and with time constraints. Typically, time is spent alone together talking; having fun; hanging out; just being together; eating; and drinking. Because it takes time and energy to arrange a meeting, caring is implied. In contrast to dating couples, whose time together is mostly social, being with other people and going out to movies and parties, single woman–married man time is mostly intimate. Concealment means that most of the activities that sustain the relationship take place in private. What there is to talk about is themselves and their relationship, rather than the movie, the party, the other people.

The world-out-there with its prescribed rules and roles, expectations and obligations can be set aside as the couple construct their own world-in-here, a world freer from social constraint and cultural definition. Expectations about how a date should act, what a potential husband should do, how a couple behaves can be set aside. The heavy bargaining and escalating expectations that attend regular male-female romantic interludes can be suspended. The interested parties, family and friends, who would normally evaluate one's relationship remain ignorant of it, mute. Because there is no culturally prescribed way to construct a single woman–married man relationship and because there is little feedback from others, the pair, relatively autonomously, alone together, can create the relationship, its boundaries and its focus:

> In the beginning, I felt like I could experiment with being someone I usually wasn't. I felt free.

> We didn't have any expectations of each other, and we didn't have to exploit each other. The relationship didn't have to have a goal. We could just be. Like friends who are lovers.

Because the partners know that their time together is circumscribed by his primary obligations, and because the clandestine

rendezvous must be arranged, expectations are high. The time together is treated as "special," "worthwhile," and "important":

> There was a purity about our relationship that has never
> existed with any other man that I have been involved with.
> I think it's that we never had much time together and we
> never wasted it fighting, arguing, or worrying about or talk-
> ing about the nature of our relationship. We just did it.
> And it was like this fantasy romantic lover. No demands
> on either side. Understanding there were limitations. It was
> a very innocent, totally nonmelodramatic kind of relation-
> ship.

> I don't think it was done consciously, but we did stop the
> clock, freeze the relationship when it was particularly roman-
> tic. It didn't have to deteriorate because of having to be in
> a day-to-day domestic situation where demands are made
> on each other that are unpleasant or mundane. It was never
> mundane. It was encapsulated.

Time together is viewed positively. Even minor annoyances can
be ignored because there is no reason to magnify them because
the relationship is, after all, time constrained. Moreover, the time
together is still thought of as safe because women believe that a
relationship with a married man will be a temporary one, and temporary relationships are judged relatively risk-free.

Unlike a few generations ago, when a temporary liaison was
dangerous, since it reduced a woman's "marketability" as a wife
and she ran a much greater risk of pregnancy, today transitory
relationships are much more common. Better, it is now frequently
argued, to experiment before marriage or remarriage, than to be
locked into a disappointing or destructive nuptial bond. Women
see relationships with married men as belonging to this category
of experimental and temporary relationships, suspended in time
and not going anywhere, a safe place to risk new ways of behaving:

I knew it was going to be a short-term relationship, and I had no intention of keeping up the relationship so I felt safe in it.

I knew from the beginning that it was going to end.

I'm willing to take a risk. I don't have to keep myself under control because it's not so dangerous because it can't go anywhere. I can forget that rational stuff—I've done that long enough.

Space and time, then, are both controlled by his marital status. Privacy and temporal constraints become the twin pillars between which the relationship is constructed. Privacy leads to semi-autonomous definitions of what the relationship should be like, and time constraints lead to valuing the time together as well as to feeling emotionally safe. Unexpectedly, but as a direct result of the man's marital status, the stage has been set for her to care about him, perhaps even to fall in love. The necessary cultural props are in place: The two are alone together.

Secrecy not only surrounds these relationships, secrets percolate within them. Since in our culture, secrets are viewed as "possessions" that are "had," "kept," and "given away," to tell a secret about oneself is to invite intimacy and to risk betrayal. Not to share secrets, though, keeps the relationship circumspect, the self, isolated.[7] Because relationships between single women and married men are carried on in private and are believed to be safe because they are thought of as temporary, ample opportunities for reciprocal self-disclosures arise. Indeed, emotional intimacy based on the sharing of secrets is situationally induced.

In those relationships which women define as "deeply and fully intimate," the feelings of closeness grow as the man talks about his life. In the process, he discloses fears and anxieties, trials and mistrials, hopes and dreams. Women listen. They offer advice, sympathy, or insight, whether the issue is his children, his job, his wife, or his mid-life passage. The specific issue is not what entices the woman. Rather, it is his apparent willingness to reveal himself, to be emotionally open, to talk:

I knew everything about him . . . Everything.

He's told me things he's never told anyone else.

In turn, the woman also talks about herself:

It was like an add-a-pearl necklace. At first he was putting all the pearls on the string, then I added some.

I let my guard down. I ended up telling him more about my life than I had told other people. I had never let a man inside me like that.

The importance of these exchanges cannot be minimized, for one of the major complaints of contemporary women is the problem of finding men they can *talk* to.[8] Contemporary women are less likely to want to just "sit and listen"; less likely to be satisfied with the "good buddy" role; less tolerant of being patronized or ignored; and more insistent on emotional intimacy and emotional equality. In a relationship with a single woman, a married man can allow himself, should he so choose, to be emotionally vulnerable. It is easier, for example, to reveal one's deepest feelings in a relationship which is readily terminated; it is safer to discard one's veneer when there is little threat of being trapped or psychologically dominated. Indeed, for aristocratic European and South American men, being in love with, and emotionally vulnerable to, one's mistress, rather than one's wife, has long been the custom for just that reason.[9] Above all, being a good listener and emotionally open is relatively easy in a hidden relationship of limited duration with time-constraints, especially since by doing so, the married man is more likely to keep his extramarital relationship.

In relationships between single women and married men the exchange of secrets is normal and routine. If there appears to be no betrayal, the trust level rises because one is telling another about his or her deepest fears and hidden agendas, and the other is listening. The more self-disclosures without apparent betrayal, the greater the trust, and the greater the subsequent feeling of self-worth:

> We are much more intimate than I have ever been with any other man. I know some secrets about his family that he has never told anybody. He was so moved that he could talk to me that he took my head in his hands and said, "I can really talk to you." He is like a friend and a lover. I feel wonderful. I respect him.

Listening to his self-disclosures gives the single woman a sense of moral rectitude and moral superiority that other elements of the relationship may not sustain. Being his trusted confidante, the single woman feels ennobled, for to be trusted with a secret means you are judged a worthy person, a moral person:[10]

> I still marvel that he considered me worthy enough to know him that well. His wife may have had his name, but I had his soul.

> I had this ethic I had created for myself about selfless love. I was going to make no demands, but the purity of my feelings for him were so terrific that it made me a good person. That was my theory.

One woman, whose lover, a devout Catholic who had told her from the beginning he would never leave his wife, thought he was the most "honest and honorable man" she had ever known. She knew how much their relationship cost him in guilt, a guilt that ennobled. He sent her a poem by Lovelace, the last two lines of which she recites from memory:

> I could not love thee half so well
> Loved I not honor more.

Not all women experience the same depth of feeling toward their married lovers. Some even desire emotional distance. Often these are women who have invested highly in their careers. But, even some of these women become more involved than they had anticipated because their relationships, to their surprise, help relieve some major conflicts in their personal and professional lives.

Although women are becoming professionals and executives, many are feeling insecure in those roles. Some fear that their "femininity" will be lost or compromised by doing "masculine" work. Others wonder whether they are really capable of doing the work or whether they are frauds. These are the doubts that pursue many upwardly mobile women. It is not success they fear so much as being found inadequate, imposters.[11] With few role models to guide her, a contemporary woman desires reassurance. Although she can discuss these anxieties with other women, and even discover they feel the same way, such knowledge may not sufficiently boost her confidence.[12] Because we live in a male-centered society, a man's positive assessment of a woman's competence and "attractiveness" is what continues to matter to most women. The man's power to build confidence, or destroy it, makes his approval the one she usually most desires.

With a married man some women find that they can risk expressing their inadequacies and fears without the threat of having them discovered by others and without the risk of getting "too" involved. They can be vulnerable and weak, a luxury many deny themselves in their professional roles. The married man who listens and builds confidence, however, creates in her more emotional attachment than she had anticipated:

I hadn't realized how powerful a force he would be in my life because I hadn't realized how much I needed a safe harbor. A place where I didn't have to know everything and make all the decisions. Me needing someone to look after me took me by surprise. That's what swept me off my feet.

Whether women are more or less resistant to emotional involvements, or more or less traditional in their attitudes and needs, the outcome is strikingly similar in kind, differing only in intensity:

Single women often enough find themselves really caring for their married lover, perhaps even find themselves in love.

Little wonder that single women grow emotionally close to their married lovers, for they have repeated occasions to share secrets freely in a context of increasing high regard for the self and the other, conditions that sociological and psychological research find consistently related to feelings of love.[13] The desire of contemporary women to feel free and safe is fulfilled in these relationships. What they are experiencing is the kind of intimate exchange we call love.[14] At this point, many women become committed to preserving the relationship, and to doing whatever is necessary to sustain it, even if that means continuing to keep its existence secret and shrouding their lives.

Committed now to continuing the relationship because she does care about him and because she does feel both "free" and "safe," an unexpected, uncomfortable, feeling arises: uprootedness. She experiences this precisely because she is in a *new* relationship that is *secret* and not socially discussed and acknowledged:

> I was in love, and I didn't know what to do about it. I hadn't planned on this. I started a journal because I needed someone—something—to help me make sense of what was happening to me.

Being in a new relationship of any kind—love, parental, work— creates a new world of meanings and associations which requires some break with the previous world. Usually that break is facilitated by talking about the new world, by having its existence socially acknowledged. We talk about our new office, our new boss, our new friends, or our new lover. Through our conversations, the new relationship begins to seem real, natural, and normal.[15] But when the new world is stigmatized and not talked about, both its existence and one's identity within it remain shaky. The feeling of dislocation can be severe.

For any new relationship to persist, the feeling of uprootedness has to be overcome. For the newlywed woman, many social supports stabilize her new identity and make the marriage seem objectively "there": the "constant conversation" with her husband; her daily exchanges with friends, relatives, associates, and tradespeople (Good Morning, Mrs. _____); letters and invitations to her as a member of a socially approved couple; the way marriage is taken for granted in the media and in her social circle; and the multitude of role models in life and fiction. None of these everyday confirmations are available to the single woman involved with a married man, however. Nor are those which validate her existence as a member of a "dating" couple. Her parents and friends are not looking him over, evaluating him, and talking about him.

One outcome of this lack of social acknowledgment is being released from having to fulfill social expectations. The new wife, after all, may have to resist having her identity swallowed up in her husband's name, and she may resent expectations that she act like a wife. But, she does not *doubt* that she is in a relationship; she is constantly reminded of her status: wife. Unlike the bride, the single woman can build her private world, suspended in time, relatively free of social definition, but she may have to struggle hard to prove to herself that her relationship with a married man really does exist.

One of the major ways she proves to herself that the relationship does exist is by imbuing objects and rituals with intense symbolic significance. Although any enduring relationship has private possessions—objects, photos, and mementos—that record and glorify the relationship, what is different about the single woman–married man relationship is that these objects carry the major burden of *proof* that the relationship *as a relationship* exists. Similar to a childless couple's cat which becomes the cherished repository for parental feelings, objects and rituals testify to the relationship's past and present. One woman's object was her bedroom, which she "redid" with her lover, choosing colors from paint samples, repainting the walls, sanding the floors, and acquiring plants and prints:

It was something I wouldn't have done by myself or for myself. We did it for ourselves. I always felt his presence.

It became *our* bedroom. We'd lie in bed and look at our poster collection and laugh at what bizarre taste we had.

Another woman saved mementos (bottle labels, television guides, ticket stubs) which she placed in a drawer. Her lover began to refer to it as "our drawer." A third woman kept a photo album that she and her lover periodically viewed together; those were "very special times when we could remember again." The bedroom, the drawer, and the photo album are private possessions of *both* the lovers, secret possessions shared in common through which they can mutually celebrate their relationship and preserve its history. Moreover, the private keepsakes remain private. They are not displayed on cocktail tables, bookshelves, and livingroom walls, nor are they talked about with others. Because they are not publicly shared, and yet carry the burden of proof, their symbolic significance is intensified.

For some women, the objects are imbued with a semisacred quality and appear to be almost enshrined. One woman keeps "their" scrapbook in a "secret place," hidden from her children, parents, and friends. She holds it and carries it as though it were an original Gutenberg; she turns its pages with extraordinary caution, fingertips alighting only at the corners, as though even her hands might sully the treasured photos. Another woman stands like a silent supplicant before a bulletin board in her bedroom. Pinned to it are a dried-out bouquet, a Valentine's Day card, movie ticket stubs, and some postcards. The bulletin board is placed so she sees it as she turns off her light. Both women behold their objects with reverence as though they are performing a sacrament.

Some women have less tangible ways of affirming they are in a relationship. These include shared rituals, such as the use of private languages and jokes, secret phone codes, and the celebration of anniversaries. Frequently emphasized are the predictability and stability of these shared rituals, underscoring their significance as testimonials that a relationship with a past and a present exists:

We knew we would always have Tuesday nights. It became a standing joke between us to scoff at the Monday Blues people and the T.G.I.F.'ers. Monday was great because the next day was Tuesday—and after Tuesday, who *needs* Friday?

He wrote me every day at the same time I was writing him. Like we were really together.

We had all kinds of anniversaries we celebrated—our first date, our first kiss, the first time we stayed together. The first year we celebrated them every month—we called them "month-iversaries." We'd find special things to celebrate— like our first crab dinner-versary, our first petunia sighting "versary." It got so we would invent lots of "versaries." I began to record them just for fun in a daybook I bought. He'd write things in it too.

Unlike standard marriages, where erotic love and romance are replaced by children and household property, the idea of eternal romance is generated in single woman—married man relationships. Collecting photos, letters, and souvenirs and creating secret languages and private jokes confirm the existence of the relationship. Celebrating the relationship with reverence toward objects and the invention of "anniversaries" help freeze the relationship as a romantically erotic one. Rather than simply exchanging secrets about the self, the couple now "owns" a set of private possessions and "has" a set of *mutually* valuable secrets. As a result, a new kind of intimacy arises: The single woman feels "attached to" the married man; she feels she is "a part of" a relationship. Belongingness: This feeling, too, like the one arising from self-disclosures, is one we associate with being in love.[16] Could this be love, then?

Many women at this point in their relationships are experiencing the pleasures of emotional intimacy, the sharing of secrets, and the feeling that one is a valuable, good person. They are also experiencing the pleasure of belongingness—of having mutually created private jokes and languages, and secret possessions. "We two against the [primary] world." Self-disclosure and belongingness, freedom and safety—these are so central to what we call love that even some of the most emotionally controlled of women are taken up short, for this *could* be love. Whatever it is, it feels good. It certainly has not been anticipated. For it to continue, though, the tension between wanting to reveal it and needing to conceal it must be attended to, for life in the second world from here on is unlikely to be all romance and light.

Chapter Five

CONCEALING AND REVEALING

T HERE IS A CERTAIN AMOUNT OF PRESTIGE involved with being in love, since love is associated with being beautiful and desirable. So, when a woman is in love, she wants to tell the whole world, to shout it from the rooftops. She wants the admiration rightfully due her. But when a woman is in love with somebody else's husband, that feeling is tainted; the whole world is a narrow one, the shout has to be muffled, and the rooftops are barricaded. Even if she is reluctant to claim that she is in love, if she has a relationship that satisfies her, she will want to talk about it, perhaps even brag about it.

The tension between concealing the relationship, protecting it from discovery by the "wrong" persons, and revealing the relationship, telling significant others about it, escalates: The more important the relationship, the greater the tension—the greater the need to protect its existence and the greater the need to sing its virtues. This tension can come to dominate the conversations between the couple. Who can know? What can they know? What risks can we take? The once seemingly ideal intimacy now has to be negotiated in the context of concealing and revealing. Angers, disagreements, fears, and ambivalences develop, as does the intensity of the intimacy.

Concealing the relationship has a number of advantages: it permits emotional intimacy without excessive demands; it gives women some freedom from social and sexual constraints; it insulates the relationship from external judgments. He has not been subject to the critical eyes and tongues of her family and friends. No one has had the opportunity to tell her, for example, that this man she thinks is great is an adventurer, and that this relationship that she thinks is unique is a replay of an old pattern. Most importantly, if she does not know him in any other context, he can lie about anything and everything if he wishes—and so can she. Her biography can be invented, she can be the woman she wants to be; his biography can be invented, he can be the man she wants him to be.[1]

Although the need for secrecy has been rooted in his marital status, it has worked for her as well. She becomes committed to keeping the relationship hidden. To accomplish this, women use four major concealment strategies: withdrawing, compartmentalizing, cloaking, and fictionalizing. Although a particular woman may light upon one of these as her favored strategy, a woman may use all or most of them at some point in her relationship, particularly if the relationship goes on sub rosa for years.

These strategies permit women to exist fairly successfully in both their primary and secondary worlds. Ironically, they are strategies which deepen the sense of intimacy and commitment to the relationship, because they decrease the opportunities for publicly testing the relationship and/or increase her dependence on it. Simultaneously, the liaison is hidden and the woman's investment in it is heightened.

In any relationship, when love is new, the new love takes precedence over previously established routines. Lovers want to spend time with each other, to suspend other relationships, obligations, and intrusions. But after a while, they come out of their twosome retreat and seek confirmation of their couplehood from others. They become acknowledged as a pair in the lives of their family, friends, and associates. What is different about a single woman–married man relationship is that the withdrawal from family, friends, and associates does not abate. *Withdrawing* becomes the routine:

While he was living with his wife, I refused to do anything public with him. Lunches were okay. But no public relationship. That went on for two and a half years.

Not only does the couple remain sequestered, but the woman may find that she, herself, is retreating from normal social intercourse as well. If she identifies herself as a part of a renegade couple, it is not a large step for her to withdraw by herself from regular social activities:

I find myself arranging my whole life around his, deciding when I can go out and when I should stay home. I don't see as much of my women friends either, because I want the time free after work to be with him, even though I get angry at arranging my life around his.

Although the woman may upbraid herself for choosing to limit her social life, if her feelings for him are stronger than her anger toward herself, her world will stay narrowed. If she is dependent upon his phoning her, she may have an additional incentive to alter her daily rounds in order to "be available":

Usually, I would let him make the first move to reach me, which meant I tried to be home a lot. I'd rush out to the store and back. That sort of thing. I let him have the initiative. It was safer that way.

So effective can withdrawing be that a woman may stop being the person she was. She gives up parts of her identity:

I don't think I realized how much I had given up until I got out of it. Even my sister said, now I'm back to being who I was—how much of me had vanished.

In a normal relationship you usually don't have to give up who you are. In my relationship, even though I was still an individual, I gave up my family, my identity, my culture, the theater, the arts, dance, reading, laughing—I really did.

Withdrawing limits the amount of interaction with old friends and family, but even more saliently, it changes the character of those interactions. Since the risk of revealing her secret is increased should she share anything of importance about her life, the conversations she has with her friends and family become more distant, cold, shallow. She no longer trusts herself to discuss anything in her life, for fear she will reveal everything about her life. Thus, her previous support network shrivels:

> I didn't tell my family. I didn't share it with friends. I even closed off my counseling channels. I stopped going to therapy. It was natural to close off those channels because he did a lot of it for me. I just repressed my life. I didn't talk about anything to anyone.

By using the withdrawing strategy, the single woman loses her support network, and she reduces her chances of making new friends and of meeting new men. Opportunities for a different liaison are effectively ended while she "arranges" her life around his:

> Sometimes, I think I'm wasting my life waiting for him. I'm waiting for him when I could be maybe meeting someone else. He says if something comes up, go ahead and make other plans, don't wait for him. But I want to be with him.

If a woman retreats further into social and emotional isolation, the one person who does remain in her life is her married lover: He does, *de facto*, become her "whole life." Her strategy of withdrawing intensifies her dependence on the relationship, her commitment to it, and her concomitant feelings of love. He is her one "true" intimate. In some ways, she becomes like a traditional wife, removed from circulation, at home, waiting. Other Women can become withdrawn somewhat easily, almost unconsciously, because waiting and being available is consistent with their early socialization as females, and that socialization is difficult to disregard.

Withdrawing deepens a woman's commitment because it isolates her from other people and different opportunities. But another strategy, *compartmentalizing*, may be chosen because it allows the woman to stay actively involved in more parts of her life, because her liaison is separated from them. In general, the contemporary woman is quite adept at putting each major role she plays into a different airtight cubicle. For survival and success she has learned to forget about home when she leaves for work and to forget about the office when she gets home.[2] Concentration on one full-time job is enough, and she senses that even something as trivial and acceptable for her male colleagues as keeping pictures of their children on their desks may be interpreted in her case as a lack of dedication to the company, or as an invitation to treat her as a mother rather than as a professional, or as a plaintive reminder that she has a life elsewhere. Better to separate the worlds. For such women, placing a lover into another separate category is an easy extension of her compartmentalizing life strategy:

They were all very separate. My parents don't live here. The community where I work is fifty miles away from where I live. He lived in a different town and we could meet halfway. My sons were used to seeing me going away on business trips.

For a woman who has an out-of-town lover, this strategy dovetails especially well with the rest of her life. Because the lover is not closely tied to her geographically, it is easier to separate him from the rest of her activities:

We see each other about once a month or every six weeks. He writes and phones three–four times a week. Distance

is good because it helps to maintain the fantasy, not to have
to see him in everyday life.

Compartmentalizing, whether through an act of will or a fact
of geography, works, because women feel they can exercise control
over both their worlds:

> Because I know I can close the door when he leaves—because
> the relationship does not control my whole life, I can give
> and get more from it and from everything else in my life.

> I'm the kind of person who likes to do whatever I am doing
> very intensely, and I don't like a lot of distractions. When
> I see him, that's what I want to do, and when I'm working
> on a layout, that's what I want to do. I don't like to be
> pulled in different directions.

For the while, grown accustomed to never being a "whole self,"
to separating her various roles, she believes she has the "best of
all possible worlds." The tensions generated by splintering off parts
of herself, by dividing up her life like the spoils of war, are ignored
or downplayed. She judges the energy it takes to keep her various
roles insulated from one another as less demanding than trying
to integrate them.

Not all women can successfully compartmentalize their lovers.
For women whose routine social or work life overlaps with their
married lover's, the *cloaking* strategy is likely to be used. Like spies
and members of secret organizations, the lovers act *as if* the time
they spend together is explainable by their mutual work interests
or old friendship.[3] The women believe others attribute the time
she openly spends with her lover as conventional, legitimate activity. For example, one woman whose lover was her supervisor routinely stayed late at the office, took "business" trips with him,
and called him at home regarding "work-related matters." Another
woman, who team-taught with her married lover, spent considerable public time with him preparing for class, grading, and reviewing.

A third has her "old friend" over, ostensibly to "repair things" around the house.

But perhaps the most frequent cover-up is the "business lunch." Being together in the day, in public, eating, is a common way in which single women spend time with their married lovers. Doing business at lunch is a long-time tradition between men, and is becoming more common between men and women as more women move into managerial positions. There is a double bind here, though. Single women think that others will assume that she and her lover are having a "man-to-man" talk, a "client to customer" or "colleague to colleague" dialogue. But because exchanges between men and women are generally eroticized, others are likely to interpret the luncheon as a noontime tryst even when it is not.

By using the cloaking strategy, the single woman can be with her married lover fairly frequently and openly. If they have been workmates or friends, cloaking permits her to maintain her usual stance toward him. By not altering their daily behavior, she believes suspicion can be averted:

He's gone from home a lot. The company expects me to be with him, as an aide. So, there has been no change in his patterns.

We were research associates together. Everyone thought, I am sure, that we were so close because we worked together so closely.

We spend evenings together. He calls home and says he's working late. She's used to it.

The cloaking strategy permits the two to spend public time together that she believes camouflages the real nature of the relationship. It also deepens the sense of "we-ness" because they share a secret. Moreover, a woman can reveal to others her positive regard for her "co-worker" or "friend," and she can legitimately know things about him such as his work schedule, his home phone number, his children's names. Her private life can be somewhat integrated with her public one, but the amount of actual overlap remains disguised.

In addition to cloaking, compartmentalizing, and withdrawing, women use a fourth major strategy to conceal their relationships: *fictionalizing.* Equivocating and lying, by omission and commission, about his marital state is common:

> He met my family—they thought he was divorced and was courting me.

> The people at work know I'm dating a man, but they don't know he's married.

> I'm lying to the children. They think he's divorced. It's difficult for me because they are getting attached to him.

> I tell people he's divorced.

More elaborate fictions are also invented. Women may simply lie to others about what they did with their weekends and vacations and lie about the reasons for their emotional states. Sometimes a fictitious lover, a socially acceptable relationship, is invented. Most often elaborate fictions are used at work, where the social time and depth of involvement with co-workers is limited, but where some talk of one's personal life is expected. In this respect, Other Women are similar to gay men, lesbians, and others who are in nonconventional relationships.

Women who simply lie can find themselves separated from others, fearful of betraying themselves, and moving into greater isolation and dependence upon their married lovers. Women who create a fictitious lover feel the relief of being able to talk about their real one in a concealed way, but having found that solution may limit their need to consider a different relationship. In either case, fictionalizing intensifies the woman's dependency and psychologically reduces her options.

What these strategies—withdrawing, compartmentalizing, cloaking, and fictionalizing—share in common is that they sustain the intimacy while concealing it. The acts required to conceal the relationship create new mutual secrets, limit external testing of the relationship, increase her dependency, and reduce her opportunities for alternative relationships.

As her feelings escalate, though, so does the tension between wanting to talk about her relationship and wanting to keep it secret. Often enough, at this point, the couple plays at being found out. They engage in *gambling*. Risking being caught by playing public hide-and-seek dramatizes the relationship; turns it into a thriller romance. She can be Lauren Bacall; he, Humphrey Bogart. The couple might meet at a neighborhood bar, or he might drive her home from work, or they might take a trip together, or he may escort her to some special event.

The existence of the relationship is still concealed from significant others. But through being together in public, going on trips together, the possibility of revealing it to strangers emerges. Strangers are important because one can act "normal" in front of them, or make up stories, and not be held accountable.[4] Strangers can confirm, admire their relationship, and then move on; they can provide a continuous new source of acknowledgment and validation; they can substitute for the friends, family, and associates who are ignorant of the relationship.

But since usually it is the wife who is to be kept ignorant, sometimes gambling enterprises are devised that specifically risk her discovering the relationship. One husband has the Other Woman call him at home. If his wife answers, she claims she is a (bogus) client's secretary and leaves an encoded love message which the wife duly delivers. Another man buys a concert ticket for the Other Woman the same night he and his wife are going. During intermissions, the lovers signal each other. One man phones from home:

Last night he called me twice from home. He told me he loved me; his voice was lowered a bit. I said, "Are you home alone?" and he said, "No."

For the gambling to be fun, the element of risk must be present, but the stakes not so high that he could lose everything in one hand. The basic underlying belief, like that of all inveterate gamblers, is that they are somehow invincible, that even if they cheat, they will not be caught:

> He wants me to fly into his little town. He's playing at being found out. He's taking risks.

> We go to concerts and plays together. I think he is trying to get caught. He denies it. He says that people would think that if we were having an affair, it would be clandestine. He says the best way to cover up is to be out in the open.

Highly significant, the married man, not the single woman, decides when and how the gambling will be done and toward whom the games will be directed. Men, in general, are more willing to take risks than women.[5] This is one of those basic gender differences. Because he decides what risks to take, though, she has less control over the outcome of the relationship.

But even more important, the way the married man chooses to gamble allows him to cover all his bets, yet gives the illusion of taking great risks. If his wife does not find out, he wins because he keeps the Other Woman and can continue to display the liaison publicly, if he so chooses. If his wife does find out, his losses are still containable. He may have to terminate this particular extramarital relationship, which may grieve him or which may be something he has wanted to do anyway, but it will not preclude his starting a new liaison. Or, if he wants to get out of his marriage, publicly humiliating his wife may force her to seek a divorce. With no-fault divorce common today, he will not be legally or economically punished for his infidelity. The possible permutations and the latent gains, for the husband, are many.

Gambling enhances feelings of intimacy because of the dangers implied, the romance engendered. The Other Woman may interpret his behavior as "risking everything," a testament to his devotion. Even a little bit of gambling goes a long way toward creating a mystique around the relationship, of seeing it as impervious, of having it challenged by discovery, and surviving, as though fate were on their side. And it allows the woman to feel that she is a part of a "regular" couple, out in public doing the things that couples normally do.

Publicly gambling with being found out, though, is not wholly satisfying for the single woman, because it does not fulfill her need to *talk* about her relationship to important people. Gender differences between women and men pervade even this aspect of the relationship. Just as his definition of friendship involves doing things together, risking being found out by playing around in public is *his* way of announcing the relationship. So her definition of friendship means intimate talk, and wanting to tell significant others in private about it is *her* way of announcing the relationship. His way is public; her way is private.

Her impulse to tell others grows stronger as the relationship continues and her emotional commitment intensifies. Should she hide her secret world from friends and family, the isolation can be great and painful. The high potential for pain is similar to any woman's who conceals deep secrets, whether it be a battering husband, an abusing father, alcoholism, drug dependency, or lesbianism. To tell is a risk, but not to tell is a greater one in terms of pain and isolation.

Like the process of "coming out," revealing oneself as a homosexual or lesbian, the process of coming out as an "Other Woman" is not easily accomplished. As gays and lesbians have experienced, as well as persons who date across racial, age, or social class lines, one is not quite sure how others will respond to a nonstandard relationship; what insults will be tossed; what "therapeutic" interventions will be proposed; what gossip will go on behind one's back; what supercilious "I told you so" comments will arise, when the relationship is going poorly. Moreover, the process of coming out is never over.[6]

Because the normal world is the maritally coupled one, people assume, unless told otherwise, that a single woman is involved with a single man or wants to be. To be "out" as an Other Woman requires announcing it anew in each new space, to each new person. But once she has confided her secret, it has a life of its own. She no longer has control over herself as the topic of other people's conversations. Her status as mother, daughter, friend, or co-worker may pale as people come to associate her whole identity, the explanation for her successes and failures, her ups and downs, with her *spoiled status:* that of the Other Woman.[7]

Because the Other Woman status is seen as a peculiar and stigmatized one, coming out is an arduous process for most single women. By and large, a woman chooses to tell those people whom she imagines will be the least judgmental and the most supportive. But since she shares her secret world with another, her married lover, she does not have total control over who knows what and when they know it. Family, friends, and work associates are people who might be told about the relationship. The married man and the Other Woman, though, choose different significant others and different ways to reveal the liaison.

Of all of a woman's *family* members—parents, siblings, children—she is most likely to talk to her sister about her relationship. Sisters have a special relationship to one another. They are of the same generation, are the same sex, and have been reared by the same parents, so they share common generational, cultural, and familial histories. Because they are related to one another, but not responsible for or highly dependent upon each other, as children are on parents, they are more likely to accept each other's foibles and less likely to generate guilt or demand change in each other:

> At first my sister was sort of judgmental, and concerned that his wife might shoot me, but now she is tolerant. Now that she has met him she likes him, but she doesn't understand.

> I wanted him to meet my sister. She came from out of town. She knew he was married.

> The first one I finally told was my sister.

A "good sister" is like a "good friend," but more than that because of the kinship ties. She is likely to be sensitive to her sister's moods and knowledgeable about their parents' reactions and responses. If necessary, she can find a satisfactory "cover" for her sister that explains her absences and moods. This is often necessary, because telling one's parents is difficult, if not impossible:

I had tried bringing the topic up with Mom and Dad, just asking how they would feel if my married brother had a girlfriend and how they would feel if I were dating a married man. Mom said her concern would be that I would get hurt. I tried to expand on it, but she changed the topic.

My mother knew about him and the child and Missy, but she didn't know he was married. She just thought they were living together and had an illegitimate child.

My mom has met him and I just try to play him down as just a good friend. She hasn't asked a lot of questions about it, but you know if she really thought about it, she would wonder why I was home on Saturday nights. But I play like he is just a really good friend.

No doubt the parents are conspirators in their own ignorance. They want to know that their daughter is "happy," is seeing a "nice man," but they do not want to know the truth. Like the parents of gays and lesbians, they would rather believe almost anything other than the reality, because they blame themselves, feel guilty, for having reared a child "without sense or morals." It is the rare parent who can accept that a daughter is involved with a married man, and that parent is usually the mother, especially a mother who has been divorced:

Mom and I have always been real close. I'm living with her now and we're more like friends. I've told her about it. She understands. She told me she dated a married man for a while, too, after the divorce. I thought she had.

Little is known about relationships between divorced women and their daughters, although it is highly likely that, without the presence of a father/husband, a special closeness and camaraderie develop. As the daughter grows up, it is likely she will have experiences with men similar to her mother's. Since the demographic constraints continue to affect succeeding generations of women, mothers and grown daughters may become more sisterlike, comparing their problems in finding an agreeable relationship with a man.

But if her sisters and her sisterlike mothers are her potential allies, her children are her conscience. Women do not want their children to know that the man their mother is dating is married, although they tend to be vague on the reasons for their silence:

I don't think they would understand.

It didn't seem necessary for them to know.

I just didn't tell them.

Underlying their reticence are a number of beliefs: that children cannot be trusted with a secret; that telling them his marital status is a secret engraves its "wrongfulness"; that children are judgmental; that the relationship will be interpreted as a sexual one by the children; or that the relationship will set a "bad" example. At base, if a single woman felt that her relationship with a married man was acceptable, her children would be told.

In contrast to a woman's sheltering her children from the truth is the common pattern of her married lover choosing to tell his older sons about the relationship:

He told his thirty-year-old son that I was his girlfriend. He wants to meet me. His seventeen-year-old son asked him if he had a girlfriend, and he said yes. His son said he didn't blame him. So his kids are somewhat supportive.

He wanted me to go to lunch with him and his twenty-year-old son. We didn't tell him in words about us, but he could tell by the way his father was acting toward me. Very solicitous. Touching me.

Men who tell their sons are communicating their approval of extramarital relationships and, perhaps, their devaluation of marital fidelity. Fathers confiding in sons, indeed introducing their sons to their Other Women, display themselves as sexually competitive and sexually successful men. Getting a son's approval creates a special "man-to-man" bond between father and son, an alliance that excludes the wife/mother.

Although a single woman may tell family members about her relationship, the most likely persons she will confide in are her close women friends. After all, that is what close women friends do—talk about their lives. Often, because women had not expected the relationship to gain such importance in their lives, they talked about it with friends somewhat offhandedly, as a lark, a new friendship, or a puzzle. When the relationship deepens, however, it may be difficult to continue talking about it because doing so seems like a violation of a trust between herself and her lover:

I stopped talking about him to my friends because I thought it disloyal.

Now it's heavy, it's serious. I don't want to talk about it.

Should a woman decide to reveal her relationship and her feelings about it to friends, she may find that they have had or are having similar attachments. As women in the past have talked about their pregnancies and births, women friends today are talking to each other about their married lovers:

A friend from college came to visit and she figured it out. It turned out she was an "other woman" too, and that was how she could tell. We'd talk every weekend, share books about it, and we'd talk about points in the book and that stuff. And we talked about highs and lows. Because, sometimes she'd call and I'd be really high on the relationship and other times I'd say, "God, break, get out, save yourself the pain I'm in right now."

My best friend asked me if I liked being single again and I said, "Wow, it's free, it's wonderful. All the taboos are gone." And then I said something about I've even considered having an affair with a married man. And she jumped up and said, "Don't do it!" I realized I'd hit a nerve, and that's when she told me about herself.

My friend said she was watching me very closely to see how my relationship went because she was holding off but didn't think she would much longer.

Single women are likely to talk to other *selected* single women about their relationships, women they are especially close to or women they suspect are similarly involved. One of the outcomes of this is that single women can create a support system for themselves among other single women. The women listening, having been there themselves, empathize. But another outcome may be that single women become more isolated from married ones. Rarely trusting that a married woman would understand, much less condone, a liaison, which might under certain circumstances threaten her own marriage, the distance between the single and married worlds becomes even greater.

The single woman has control over what friends she chooses to tell, but no power over who her lover chooses to talk to. Similar to dating relationships and to the process of getting involved in the first place, the married man may let a "good buddy" in on the relationship, let him "stand in" for him. The function of her friends is to be sympathetic listeners, whereas the function of his is to be a public adjunct to the relationship. Because she spends time with his buddy, though, he may become her confidante:

One Friday night when we were out, he said that his friend John was going to stop by. Well, I felt a little uncomfortable at first but after that, sometimes John and I would just sit there and talk at the bar. I would say, "I know this is wrong and whatever," and he would say, "If you love him—and it is obvious that he loves you—isn't that what counts?"

Casting his best friend in the role of "soothsayer" and "safe" male escort provides her with another male ear and the illusion that it is an independent one. Here is someone who also cares about her lover, who thinks he is special; here is someone to whom she can sing his virtues and someone who will listen to her ambivalences; and here is someone she can be with while her female friends are out with their lovers, or out "looking," something she has no desire to do.

Men can also choose to make their relationship known at work, a choice which most women preclude because they feel they lack control over their work lives and are potentially vulnerable. Their abilities can be underrated and their success attributed to their sexual wiles, rather than to their hard work and talent. Whereas *having* a "mistress" may be grounds for approval, *being* a mistress may be grounds for disapprobation:

> There were no women at my rank in my unit. I couldn't talk to either my subs or my supers. I wouldn't have dreamed of talking to the men in the office. They were trying to undercut me enough as it was.

For a woman to talk to anyone at work about her relationship can be risky, because women sense little control over their work lives. If they do confide in others at work, these are usually persons who are considered equals and friends:

> All the girls in the office are young and unmarried. We talk a lot about our affairs and men. I think we're so open with each other because we're all similar. College-educated, underemployed, and looking for a different job.

Men can choose to make their liaison public at work without too much fear because they will not be condemned for it and because they usually can keep their wives away from their work setting and involvements. A husband has traditionally had the power to define the role his wife plays in his life.[8] For older, intact marriages, that power has not abated. For new marriages, if there are young children in the home, his wife will be taking care of them should he *choose* not to. The children's needs and schedules will dictate his wife's comings and goings.[9] What this means is that most husbands are rather free to come and go, and to decide how much their wives know about their work and, therefore, who among work associates can be privy to their extramarital relationships:

> He called and asked me to come to Sparky's Bar, and I thought he was there by himself. I met four or five people who worked for him and he had quite a bit to drink and he was hanging on me and they all knew. I felt a little self-conscious because I felt like they thought, Oh, she's the "other woman." I worried about what they would think of him. But I kind of felt good that he wanted them to meet me.

> His secretary must know. As soon as she hears my voice, before I identify myself, she's out looking for him.

> All the men in the business group [in another town] knew that I was Edward's mistress, but the wives didn't. The wives hated me. They hated their husbands because Edward treated me so well. We would go out and they would say, "Why can't you treat us like Edward treats his wife?" They thought we were married. Edward was wonderful. Everyone knew our relationship was special.

Coming out to family, friends, and work associates is a continuing process. The costs of staying concealed are psychologically and socially many, but so are the risks of revealing. In either case, the strategies which women use strengthen their bonds with their married lovers, for they are selective in how they conceal the relationship and to whom they reveal it. Although she lacks control over her lover's risk-taking and over whom he tells, his decisions, by and large, seem to enhance her feelings about him. Believing he is risking everything for her by allowing her to know his good buddy, meet his business associates, or even receive the "blessings" of his sons, helps legitimate her position and justify his.

Concealing and revealing strategies are essential because her lover is a married man. Her life with him is intricately connected to his life with his wife. Like it or not, then, the Other Woman has to deal with that reality and with her feelings about his wife.

Chapter Six

HIS WIFE

IN HER MARRIED LOVER'S LIFE, there is another woman. He lives with this woman, has children with her, shares property with her, and has a past, a present, and a future with her. She is not just any woman. She is his wife.

Liaisons between single women and married men are obviously shaped by the fact that he is married. Because there is a wife, their world has been circumspect and circumscribed, romantic and isolated. His wife affects this world and she has the potential to ruin it. She is a powerful figure and as such can inspire strong negative feelings—guilt, jealousy, hostility—in the Other Woman. These feelings must be managed, because they threaten to destroy the relationship if left unchecked.[1]

Strong cultural messages assert that a woman having a sexual relationship with another woman's husband is immoral and should feel guilty. Depending on the reference group, the transgression is variously labeled a sin, a grievance, or a breach of sisterhood. Contrary to societal expectations, though, contemporary women rarely *express* guilt over their involvements with married men.[2] The scarlet letter has faded:

The wife was his problem. If he wanted to lie, that was on his conscience. I had no contract with her.

As far as I was concerned most of the wives were on their way out anyway. They weren't the sit-at-home kind. They had careers. So I wasn't really doing anything to hurt the relationship. I have no reason to feel guilty.

I didn't feel guilty. What the wives don't know won't hurt them.

Since women have been socialized to assume responsibility for failing children, failed marriages, and fallen souffles, it is striking that, in this case, so many aver so little responsibility. Whether some or even most Other Women are repressing guilt is not the issue here. It is rather that women do not describe themselves as guilty and thus do not burden their relationship with its weight. Guilt has the potential to erode one's self-respect and provoke resentment toward the person inspiring it, in this case the lover. One way to avoid these dangers is to *deny culpability*.

There is much in contemporary social mores and attitudes to support her view of herself as blameless. In the light of divorce trends and serial marriages, it is easy to emphasize that being married is not a permanent status and that the marriage may not last regardless of extramarital involvements. One Other Woman said:

The line between marriage and nonmarriage seems more ephemeral nowadays. Maybe, if he's married now, it doesn't mean he'll be married six months from now. Maybe he's single now, and in six months he'll have gotten married. It's a continuum.

A new consciousness of self, arising out of the human potential movement and reinforced by post–World War II affluence, asserts furthermore that the happiness and growth of the individual is of primary importance. If that happiness means overturning a marital commitment to fidelity, for example, that is regrettable, but it is not wrong.[3] According to modern psychologies, each individual is a self-contained human being, not in this life to satisfy anyone other than his or her self. Consequently, the idea that a husband "belongs" to his wife, that he is one of her possessions acquired along with the wedding china and silver, is passé. If a single woman doubts this, begins to feel guilty, and seeks counseling from a therapist or a minister, she is likely to be released from her guilt, because the counselor, trained in a new psychology, will emphasize the Other Woman's own well-being and fulfillment:

> I talked to my minister and he was very supportive. He saw a lot of good points. He was very open-minded. I was feeling very bad about this and I thought this was really wrong, but he said he could see how people got caught up and how it wasn't my fault.

It is more than changing attitudes toward the inviolability of the marital bond, and more than a therapeutic philosophy that condones extramarital relationships, however, that helps Other Women feel nonculpable.[4] For, in addition to the new social forces, the women can look at how their own relationships began and developed. For the most part, they got involved through no conscious, volitional act of their own. They did not choose the relationship, nor did they initiate it. Once involved, moreover, they had not expected to be "swept away."[5] According to our larger social ethic, people are absolved, relatively, of guilt if their intentions are unassailable.

Not feeling culpable, then, is a first-line defense against guilt, a necessary defense if the relationship is to persist. By investing energy in claiming her innocence, though, she is continuously reminded of the societal presumption of her guilt.

As the relationship progresses, specific kinds of guilt feelings can emerge such as "spending his wife's money," "keeping him away from the kids," "changing him," or volitionally *staying* in the relationship. One way to waylay these blameworthy feelings is to *deny that his wife exists.*[6] Since the husband is the primary source of information about his wife, he can establish that for all conversational purposes she is nonexistent:

> He told me that he would not talk about his wife, and as far as I was concerned she did not exist, and that she would never know about me. He said those were the rules. He set the conditions and I accepted them.

> He carefully omits any reference to her. Even when he discusses trips they have been on, he will use the first person singular.

The Other Woman can also, on her own, refuse to acknowledge his wife's existence:

> His wife just doesn't exist. She isn't.

> I didn't know her first name and I made it a point not to know it. I didn't want it to become that personal. I didn't want her to have a name.

> I don't want to know her because then I would have a relationship with her. Friendship is a contract too. It would make it too complicated; the relationships would be in conflict.

Women, as we have seen, emphasize the importance of friendship. Friendships between women are viewed as having certain ethical dimensions, such as openness, vulnerability, and equality. Having a relationship with a friend's husband violates the canons of female friendship; it is "tacky" and "complicating" because it is impossible to have an honest, open relationship with his wife. Knowing his wife's name or knowing intimate details about her can violate an Other Woman's sense of propriety between women. But not knowing the wife—refusing to acknowledge her existence, preventing her from becoming a living, real person—sidesteps these problems. A logical chain of thought exonerates the Other Woman:

If *his* wife does not exist, she cannot have feelings; if she does not have feelings, she cannot be hurt; and if she cannot be hurt, there is no reason to feel guilty:

> I always have to deal with my own sense of walking on someone else's territory. So I try not to give his wife too much reality. If his wife is not a real person and his kids are not real people and it's not really their daddy whose money I'm spending and who I'm sleeping with and keeping away from home, then I don't have to deal with my conscience. It's my way of not feeling guilty.

Avoiding guilt by denying the existence of the wife is similar to avoiding guilt about poverty by denying that hungry children and the poor do exist as individuals with faces, names, and personalities. However, it is much more difficult for the Other Woman to sustain her denial of her lover's wife as a real and feeling person, because her lover is a constant and present reminder to the contrary. Despite her best efforts, her success in denying the wife's existence is likely to be tried.

Denying his wife existence serves another end besides coping with guilt. If there is no wife, the Other Woman has greater freedom to play out her own fantasy in the relationship. The liaison, not his wife and marriage, can be the focus and concern. One does not have to juggle multiple and potentially conflicting feelings that may detract from or subvert the main drama, the single woman–married man relationship. Banishment of the wife from the clandestine world keeps the lives parallel and separate. As a result, the Other Woman is more likely to feel good about herself and her relationship because she sees herself as part of a couple and not as one point in a triangle.

A total separation of the two worlds is not always possible, however, because sometimes the single woman knows the wife. If their relationship is a fleeting, incidental one, the single woman can treat his wife in a casual manner. Feelings do not have to be attributed to her any more than feelings are attributed to other occasional actors, such as the food vendor, meter reader, or grocery store cashier:

His wife worked for the government too, but in a different office. I'd call him at home and talk to her. I just thought of her as another employee.

I was in his travel agency when she came in to get some tickets. After she left, he told me who she was. It didn't bother me.

To be so indifferent to a major person in her lover's life has some costs. When certain topics are closed to further discussion, the knowledge that the topic exists as unfinished business interferes with a fully open and honest exchange. An even more serious cost is the effect on the Other Woman of viewing the wife as an object—a nonperson. In so doing, the Other Woman reduces her own capacity for human empathy, a price which is likely to affect the tone of her current relationships with both men and women and the quality of future ones:

I am concerned that I am becoming more and more unfeeling toward other people. I wonder if I will ever be able to have open, honest relationships with women—or with other men, for that matter. I've learned how to close off that which I don't want to know about. To shut myself down. It's become who I am, the kind of person I am.

When women have more than occasional interactions with a lover's wife, it becomes impossible to deny her existence. Instead, they try to view their relationship with the married man as something separate and distinct from their relationship with his wife:

Our families spent a lot of time together. I just didn't think about him that way when we were all together, and I didn't think about her when he and I were together. It didn't seem to affect my friendship with her because she didn't know about it.

Compartmentalizing tends to reduce guilt because the woman constructs nonpermeable boundaries between the various stage sets of her life. Literally, she does not see or think about relationships or persons outside the role she is currently enacting, so that when people are offstage, they are out of the play. If compartmentalizing is successful, all feelings, other than ones related to the current interaction, are vanquished: jealousy as well as guilt. As a final bonus, that she can enjoy herself in both roles is testimony that she *should* not feel guilt.

But trying to maintain parallel relationships with her lover and his wife has its dangers. One of the primary ones is the uncertainty of whether his wife will confront the Other Woman in a public setting. One woman who worked in the same organization as her lover and his wife said:

She knows there's an "other woman," but she doesn't know it's me. I fear that she's going to confront me sometime in front of the rest of the world. I am very uncomfortable around her in public. I would be mortified if my feminist network found out.

Although a wife may be humiliated by her husband's relationship, she has the power to retaliate by humiliating—not her husband—but "his" Other Woman.[7] She can, if she chooses, and some wives have, tell everyone about the Other Woman's transgressions; the pain she is bringing to the wife; the trouble she is creating for his children; and the economic hardships she is causing for the whole family. Of course, the risk of public embarrassment to the Other Woman is always there. That is one of the reasons his wife is a threat and retains power over the relationship. But if the two women are co-workers or friends, the risks to the Other Woman are even greater—her reputation at work and with friends, and the possible loss of her job and/or friendship network. In this way, both women have the potential to hurt each other. And so it is possible to view a man's extramarital relationship as one in which a woman versus a woman profits the husband more than either of the women.

Denial of culpability, denial of the wife's existence, and/or compartmentalizing relationships go a long way toward helping the Other Woman manage feelings of guilt, despite the tensions that may remain beneath the surface. But the more involved a woman gets in such a relationship, the more likely it is for *jealousy* of his wife to become a problem:

From what he's told me, its been quite a long time [since they have had sex]. I want to believe him. When I met him, she was pregnant with the new one. She sleeps on the couch or he does, but they very rarely sleep in the same bed. But if I think about it, even though they are not close, it bothers me that they would be in the same bed because I like to have him in bed with me, just the body there. The warmth and closeness. Then I begin to feel jealous.

If you sit there and say, "Gee, I wonder if they're in bed together. Are they making love? Do I believe him when he says he hasn't slept with her in two years?"—then, you have to Novocain yourself. Blunt some things because your nerves are just right on the ends.

Because jealousy consumes much energy, provokes paranoia, and destabilizes relationships, it must be dealt with and diminished if possible. One way to reduce jealousy is to minimize her lover's relationship with his wife by attributing his marital involvement to habit, law, or custom. There is no reason to feel jealousy or guilt if the marital relationship is defined as a meaningless one:

He has to sleep with her. It's a duty. An obligation.

I know he sleeps with her, but it doesn't mean anything. It's a habit like brushing your teeth.

He and I are monogamous. His sleeping with his wife doesn't count.

Conventionalizing the sexual relationship between the husband and wife and attributing it to duty permit the single woman to desexualize it, to define it as just another role obligation, like providing food and shelter and taking out the garbage, that he has incurred by dint of being married. Sex with his wife is not sex then; it is a requirement or a chore.

Since people go to great lengths to reduce the importance of behavior they find distressing, that Other Women discount their lovers' sexual relationships with their wives is not surprising. Whether the husband is telling his lover the truth is not the issue. What is salient is that she believes him, believes that his wife does not matter to him as a sexual being. Although the clandestine relationship is built upon her lover's betrayal of his wife, the Other Woman is unlikely to imagine that he may also be betraying her— that his relationship with his wife might be more emotionally and sexually satisfying, as well as more frequent, than he lets on:

> If I thought they had a good relationship, I would be jealous. It would hurt. I guess I keep telling myself or thinking they are not close. I know they have to make love sometimes. She'd wonder otherwise.

Ironically, the rationalization of his sexual relations with his wife may encourage him to continue to perform his husbandly duties. They are now defined as a responsibility or expectation, one to which the single woman is a hidden accomplice, an aider and abetter. She can have the illusion that she is a party to their sexual life:

> We discussed this at length. Sometimes he wouldn't ejaculate so he could with her. I understood this was how it had to be. It was as hard for him as it was for me, and I think that's what made it all right.

> He told me that when he slept with her he closed his eyes and fantasized he was sleeping with me.

His ejaculatory self-sacrifices and sexual fantasy life may help her believe he does what he does with his wife in order to preserve his secret relationship:

He has to sleep with her. If he didn't, she would be suspicious.

Jealousy, then, is controlled by discounting his sexual relationship with his wife: he is not really sleeping with her; he is only sleeping with her because it is required by law and custom; he doesn't really enjoy it; or he has to sleep with her to prevent suspicion. The importance of the Other Woman's relationship to her lover overwhelms her objectivity and skepticism.

The costs of discounting his wife, though, are several, including the possibility that the Other Woman is deluding herself about the actual nature of his marriage. For a woman who finds her deepening involvement arouses hopes that he will leave his wife, discounting her role can be particularly counterproductive. If the Other Woman is convinced that he does not care about his wife, then she can believe that he will eventually leave her. She is inspired to wait for him, sometimes for years. But even if it is true that he is not enamored of his wife, it does not mean that he is willing to give up his *marriage* and *children*—issues which will concern us later.

If the single woman grows emotionally fond of her married lover or falls in love, intense negative feelings about his wife can escalate even more. One way she has to handle these feelings is to *compete* with his wife. Because of her socialization as a female, the Other Woman has been taught to think of women as competitors for the favors of men. If a woman does poorly in the competition, it is her own fault, and she may be pitied, but not respected. In competing with his wife, she is often abetted by her lover:

Men who recognize that women do go after one another use women to exploit this weakness, making oblique references and snidely setting one against the other.

When he talks about his wife, it is often by way of an implied comparison with the Other Woman; in the comparison, the Other Woman bests his wife. One career-oriented woman, whose lover was married to another career-oriented woman, said:

> I knew from his compliments to me how different I was from her. He said I was neat, sharp, interesting, and I took care of business. She bounced checks, she didn't handle the house well, she never entertained, and she wasn't at ease socially.

Another woman, small, athletic, easygoing, and Jewish, said:

> He said his wife weighs over two hundred pounds and is five feet tall. She is asthmatic and has allergies and is a bitch. She's probably a Protestant American Princess. Everything has to be just so. Nothing is ever right. She picks on him.

The implied comparison invites competition, involves the single woman in a private duel with his wife, a duel unbeknown to his wife and a duel where the husband chooses the weapons: beauty, intelligence, health, business acumen, sexuality, and empathy. He makes the rules, he picks the contestants, and he judges the tourney:

> I had never felt competitive with a woman before in my life. But, I found myself wanting him to tell me how I was different—no, not different—*better* than his wife.

The competition with his wife, a competition which the single woman perceives herself as winning, derails her jealousy and raises her self-esteem. And it also binds her closer to her married lover, for she can take sides with him against his wife. She can be his ally in *blaming* his wife.[8] Without demeaning herself, she can express her hostility toward his wife. The Other Woman's snide or angry words can be interpreted as simply being supportive of her lover, merely echoing his sentiments, and not an indication of her own stake in being thought better than the competition. Because she believes that her married lover is special, unique, and wonderful, hearing about his wife's foibles also allows her to conclude that he has a "bad wife":

She's a real bitch.

She's his cross he has to bear. Grasping and materialistic. She complains and nags. She has all this money, but she doesn't share his interests.

She knew about his first relationship and punishes him in public for it.

Residual guilt can also be eradicated by concluding that he's in a "bad marriage":

He told me how bad his marriage really was. She never told him she loved him; she wasn't passionate in bed. She was a dutiful wife and a good enough mother, but he always felt there was something lacking.

I didn't feel guilty at all. First of all they had a terrible marriage. He had to block out the way she treated him. He could not communicate and he has trouble showing emotion. She would do the most abominable things and I would get so angry. So I didn't feel any guilt at all.

He and his wife didn't talk much. I suppose after all those years they ran out of things to say to each other and maybe she was not interested any more in his work or hobbies.

By current standards, a marriage can be called "bad" if sex or passion is lacking, if the parties are only dutifully related, if they have conflicts, or if they do not talk very much to each other.

Moreover, regardless of the kind of "bad" marriage, a rationale can be constructed that defines his wife as the culpable party. This is so because wives are still held responsible for the emotional well-being of their marriages. In modern two-career marriages, the wife, for example, not the husband, can be viewed as creating the marriage problem because she has "prioritized her career":

> They had one of these busy-with-their-careers kinds of marriages, and she didn't have much time to socialize [with him]. He loved her. And he loved me. But she wasn't really working on their marriage.

Believing that his wife is "mistreating him," either by commission or omission, helps explain to the single woman why her married lover is straying, on the one hand, and yet is such a good and special person, on the other. Her cognitive dissonance is reduced and her guilt dispelled by learning that his marriage—not him—is bad or empty. He can be seen as an honorable martyr, a cross bearer, a noble man with a troubled wife. With a particularly perverse logic, then, the single woman can alleviate guilt and jealousy, channel her hostility, and raise her self-esteem by deciding she is *helping,* not hurting, the marriage:

> I felt I helped their marriage. They had lots of kids and when he had his vasectomy she thought her life was over. She really did. She was a real basket case. I helped him help her through that crisis.

> I'd feel guilty if I had wanted to steal him, but I didn't. I didn't want him. I worked to keep them together. If he had left her, I would have just turned tail and run.

> I always joke about what a favor I'm doing the wives that I'm the one he's having a relationship with because I'll make sure he goes back to her. I pride myself on the fact that all my men's marriages are still intact.

Other Women who define themselves as "helpers" have a stake in his staying married. For the most part, they do not want a permanent relationship, at this time, with an available man. Ironically, if his marriage really is vapid or self-destructive, and if she does help keep it intact, then, she is keeping her married lover from a more authentic existence. Because of the single woman's collusion, he does not have to confront the emptiness of his marriage or his duplicity:

> There was nothing left to their marriage but their house and kids. I mean, they didn't care about each other anymore, if they ever did. But he didn't want to leave her. That wouldn't have been fair. I gave him the outlet he needed to stay in his marriage.

> I don't think his marriage was really bad. Just empty. In his day Jewish women married a man because they were looking for a good father and a good provider. A man married a woman because he was looking for a good cook, who makes good chicken soup. A good mother.

Since there are underlying cultural assumptions that the husband will stray, anyway, and that he is entitled to a "good" relationship, the single woman with no intention of being a home wrecker can see herself as an ally of the wife, a therapeutic aid helping the marriage to survive. Helpers are always superior to those who need help. Helping him solve his problems with his wife elevates the Other Woman. Personally coming to the aid of the wife elevates the Other Woman even higher:

> She called me at work and started shrieking at me on the phone about being with her husband and what kind of a person did I think I was. I was sympathetic with her, tried to encourage her to get a job or something of her own interest, thinking that would make her more appealing to him. I suggested counseling.

Like a Lady Bountiful, the Other Woman can set herself above the wife, think of her patronizingly as someone in need of charity or help, which the Other Woman graciously provides. The wife's anger can be sidetracked, perhaps even subdued. The Other Woman can feel superior by remaining in control of her emotions, by not making a public scene, albeit that this definition of the situation is difficult to maintain, particularly if the wife persists in "fighting" for her husband. If she does, the Other Woman—even if she was not interested in "husband stealing"—now feels justified in venting her own hostility toward the wife, because the competition for a man has been made public. One's self-esteem as a woman is on the line:

There is a sense of triumph in competing for a man, and winning.

She was persistent. That's about all I can say for her. She's a bitch. She raised his ego fighting for him, but she didn't deserve him.

"Helping" his wife, therefore, can become the steppingstone to maligning her, just as the charitable disposition toward the poor is often a prelude to despising them because they refuse to be "helped" or, more correctly, controlled.

But perhaps the most convoluted way in which a single woman sees herself as helping is to decide that the wife is colluding in her own deception. The Other Woman "helps" the wife by sleeping with her husband, on the one hand, but not talking about it, on the other. One woman who had known the wife before her lover married her, and who had had a relationship with him before and during his marriage, commented:

I would spend every vacation and all summer with them. She was always glad to have me because when I was around he would lighten up. He wouldn't be so angry and frustrated. I was his intellectual soul mate. I was the baby's godmother.

When I was there, he slept with his wife. But what she would do was to conveniently disappear for a week, or he and I would go off together. She must have realized that this was not platonic. But he never told her. He said there wasn't any point to it. That she probably knew anyway. That she wasn't jealous. I never knew what she really did know, and we never talked about it.

Wives, like Other Women, are skilled at denying that which they do not want to see, skilled at compartmentalizing, skilled at discounting, skilled at seeing themselves as helpers and nurturers. These are, after all, methods that women, regardless of marital status, have learned to use in order to manage their lives. Yet, the Other Woman does not recognize that she and the wife have the same repertoire, and that each of them is trying to make sense of her life, each trying to cope with her relationship to a man.

When Other Women impute coconspirator status to his wife, they are overlooking some other very real possibilities. What single women are perceiving as collusion may actually be trust, trust that her husband and his friend, her husband and his co-worker, are simply what they claim to be: friends or co-workers. Other Women are also overlooking the very real possibility that a wife may purposefully choose to ignore her husband's infidelity as a strategy to preserve her marriage. A wife may feel that if she lets on, she will precipitate a crisis. If he is in the throes of esctasy, she cannot compete. By refusing to acknowledge his behavior, she escapes the complications of her husband's guilt feelings, feelings which could destroy her marriage. Her strategy may be to wait it out and publicly to deny any knowledge. "She wages a silent, secret, defensive war. Her counterattack is invisible; perfect victory is dependent on the illusion that no war had been waged."[9]

There are, of course, some major advantages that come to the single woman who convinces herself that his wife favors his infidelity. The relationship becomes simultaneously illicit and licit, socially disapproved of but acceptable to his wife. It becomes freer and safer. Guilt, jealousy, and hostility can all be suppressed: his wife wants it this way; his wife does not matter to him; his wife is not interfering with the relationship. Most important, the power of his wife is dissipated. By casting his wife into a coconspirator role, "blaming the victim," the single woman removes the moral and practical threat of the wife's making a public scene or precipitously causing the relationship to end.

One would expect that the new feminist consciousness, though, might create a different sense of guilt in women, that they would feel it unsisterly and divisive to sleep with another woman's husband. But for the most part, feminist consciousness has neither prevented women from getting involved with married men nor created new forms of guilt. What it has done is to give the Other Woman a new way to relate to the wife and to ease her own conscience.

A feminist Other Woman is aware of the social and social-psychological forces that have shaped women's destinies, and she recognizes that she and his wife have been similarly socialized and are similarly socially controlled. According to feminist beliefs, women have the right to define the parameters of their lives, to choose their own destinies. Ideologically, each woman's personal experiences and feelings are equally valid.[10] One issue, then, is to find out how the wife *would* feel about another woman being involved with her husband *prior to* the actual sexual liaison. If his wife approves, then it is all right. Contrary to feminist tenets, though, the single woman commonly garners this knowledge through the husband. She lets a man tell her how a woman feels. She lets him define his wife and she accepts his account as true:

> I asked him how she would feel about us. He told me his wife was a feminist poet who would welcome me as a sister. That she had been unwilling to have sex with him for the last decade. That she didn't care what he did as long as he left her alone. And that she was convinced he would never leave her because of his love for their son.

After having sex with this man for the first time—two years after they had met—the single woman's identification with his wife soared, but she continued to accept the man's definition of his wife's experiences:

> We made love every imaginable way. We made love all night long. But I never felt like we were really making love. He knew all the techniques, but he wasn't there emotionally. I had this "Aha!" experience about his wife. I understood her, because after that night I didn't want to have sex with him again either.

This woman believes her lover, believes that there is no sex between him and his wife because she has refused it. Whether it is true or not, she uses her own sexual experience with him as a springboard for empathizing and identifying with his wife. Once she has done that, any residual guilt or fear is awash because it is not the single woman who has caused the wife's plight; rather, her married lover is the culpable person. One way to "help" his wife, with whom she now identifies, and, incidentally, to help herself to a more satisfying relationship, is to "educate" the married man into feminism:

> I tried to raise his consciousness. He had had control of her life for fifteen years.

> He told me they had nothing in common, that she wasn't educated, had dropped out of college. I held him partly responsible for that, and I told him so. He seemed to want in her the traditional womanly things even though he said he didn't. He set her up to take care of him and the kids and their little picky house.

By raising his consciousness and believing she is helping his wife, the Other Woman derails her guilt and jealousy and raises her feelings of self-worth. She can do feminist social work among the married. For only a very occasional Other Woman does the feminist framework stretch her imagination far enough for her

er involvement as *anti-woman,* as yet another way in
en are separated from each other, and as a process
ich they come to see each other as the enemy:

His wife and I could never become close—I mean honest.
And as my feminism grew, this became an increasingly difficult issue for me. Now that I am a feminist, one of the
things that bothers me is how I empowered him against
his wife, and how I still do, even though I don't see him
anymore. I'm a weapon. Men do use women as weapons
against the one they try to hurt. I resent that very much.
It's very clear to me he uses me—he tells me his wife is
jealous, and he says that with a slight triumph.

He flaunted me to her in ways that I don't even think I
know about. Whenever they would get into a fight, he would
bring me up as an example of the perfect female. That really
outrages me. I've never done that to a man.

Once the single woman fully incorporates a feminist analysis,
the relationship is very difficult to sustain, for it is too costly to
the woman's self-esteem and self-image. Being a woman who
values women, who does not want to empower men in any way
against women or do anything that divides women, and being an
Other Woman are not compatible. She feels guilty toward the wife,
sad that the two women have been pitted against each other, and
furious at her lover. Her feminist analysis becomes a strategic element in a different kind of survival—survival as an ex–Other
Woman.

Few women, though, even feminist ones, use the ideology of
the women's movement to extricate themselves from the relationship. Rather, they use elements of the modern consciousness to
rationalize the liaisons; to reduce guilt, jealousy, and hostility. They
do not hold themselves culpable; they deny the wife's existence,
or if they cannot, they compartmentalize her; they discount her
relationship with her husband; they blame her; and they try to
help her—they try to raise her consciousness, raise his conscious-

ness, and find out how she feels about her husband's adultery. However, the fact the Other Woman self-consciously reports how she *tries* to alter her view of the situation, or selectively to perceive certain aspects of the relationship, indicates that she is aware of this as *necessary* and as what she is doing. Consequently, she is unable to deny completely what she senses as disappointing, dishonest, or deceptive about the relationship. Although the methods she uses help her sustain her relationship, they do not totally seal her off from her problems. In a relationship with a married man, a single woman can feel bad. Often.

Chapter Seven

FEELING BAD

T HE OTHER WOMAN is the *other* woman in her married lover's life. She has low priority and few privileges. She cannot count on him, and she has less power in the relationship than he. As a result, in time, almost invariably the single woman finds herself disillusioned with her married lover and disappointed in herself. She finds her imagined failure-proof world, in which an ideal relationship between a man and woman could be created, is not cast in gold, but brass, and it tarnishes. Ironically, the same conditions—time constraints, privacy, and secrecy—that have made the relationship special in the past now contribute to her feeling bad.

Something as basic as determining the frequency and extent of time spent together becomes a source of pain and resentment. The single woman loses control over how her time is spent because it is his *free* time which determines when and for how long they can be together. Wherever one looks in social relationships, the person who determines when and for how long an encounter will last is the powerful person in the relationship—the doctor rather than the patient, the priest rather than the supplicant, the teacher rather than the student.[1] Although men commonly determine the specific time and duration of their socializing with women,[2] the potential for the near total subordination of the Other Woman's time to the married man's is of qualitatively different proportions. The potential for her feeling confined, powerless, and worthless is exponential.

Part of the married man's control over the Other Woman's time emerges from the fact that he is a man, and men have traditionally had the social right to interrupt females no matter what they are doing—whether they are in light conversation or deep discourse, resting or working. Despite the women's movement, this male privilege has remained fairly well intact.[3] But because her lover is not just a man, but a married man, the Other Woman's life is frequently subjected to unexpected interruptions. His free time has priority over all of her time:

I'm never sure when he might get free. He'll call me at work, and sometimes it means I take a twenty-minute dash across town during my lunch break [and twenty minutes back across town]. I don't like it, but he's worth it.

There was a fatal flaw in the relationship. And the flaw was that he really was in charge, even when I thought I was. He would decide when to get together. When it finally came down to it, he thought I should stop what I was doing when he came over, even when he knew I had deadlines to meet. He really did not respect the importance of my work to me.

Women, in general, do not have the reciprocal right to interrupt men—in conversations, at work, in sleep. And an Other Woman has even fewer rights. Regardless of her needs, she is relatively powerless to make claims on his time:

I don't get him when I want him. If I have a need and I need to be with him and I need to be held, and if it doesn't work into his schedule, I don't get it.

I could have stayed in his area of the country for another week or so by my schedule. But he said he had psyched himself up for my departure and thought it best to follow through with his plan. I felt I had no control over it, even though I wanted to stay out there—with or without him. He was driving me to the airport. I tried to sort out how this man had gotten this power over me—the power to get me to leave.

He has the power over her, in part, because as a man he has another prerogative, the right to decide when their time together is over. She has made herself, unwittingly, dependent upon his schedule for "taking her" to the airport, and her many years of socialization into "niceness" mean his needs will have precedence over hers, his decision precedence over her spontaneity.

So culturally strong are the rights of men to control women's time that even in a long-distance relationship a married man can take charge of the Other Woman's time:

He called me every Friday night at 10 from a phone booth. He viewed it as our Friday night date. After a while, I began to resent having my freedom to come and go restricted by his phone call. He was controlling me from a distance.

I used to leave work early on Friday and go with a woman friend to the mountains, but now I don't as much. I hoard vacation and mental health days and comp hours so if he comes to town unexpectedly, I can use them then.

Being unsure whether one will be summoned or dismissed keeps one emotionally and psychologically off balance. Unable to predict what will come next, one feels less and less control over one's life. The greater the dependence—psychological, emotional, financial—the greater the feelings of powerlessness, and the less the perceived ability to alter one's life. These are techniques, in fact, used throughout history by petty tyrants and insecure supervisors. Although probably unwittingly, married men may be using these same techniques: uncertainty about keeping dates, last-minute changes of plans, unwillingness to commit to his availability while requiring hers:

> He was supposed to go with me to my high school reunion. That's something you don't want to go to alone. Then he told me he was not going to go. I was going to say, "That's okay," and not cry, but I thought I'm tired of being brave, strong, and I cried because I was disappointed. I ask myself why I tolerate it. But I keep thinking I love him so much and he doesn't need me making demands on him, too, like his wife and work.

> I don't like the aspect of getting worked in and then you get cancelled a lot and that's tough. I'm never sure when he can go and when he will cancel out. And there are times like I can't go on. I can't put up with any more, but I just feel so strongly toward him.

Abdicating control of her time arouses anger, resentment, disappointment, and depression. Given these negative feelings, why does the Other Woman allow her married lover to dictate her use of time? Why do women who may be independent as wage earners and friends arrange their time schedules around their married lovers'? Partly it is because they grow very fond of these men, as they continue to testify: Losing him is perceived of as more painful than losing control of their days. But even before women become romantically involved, or for those women who maintain some emotional distance, men still take charge of the time spent together because women assume that they will and should. Women have been socialized to accept men's time-controlling behavior as normal male behavior. At first, it is exciting to be called, and shortly after it feels like a benign expression of concern, fondness, and caring.

Once she has accepted his responsibility for when they meet or talk on the phone, the pattern has been set. Unless she specifically takes issue with this, he will maintain the privilege. And even if she does challenge him, he is likely to resist her redefinition of the situation. If he continues to exercise control over the moments of her life, then, he can encroach on the days, months, years as well, for there are no norms about where to draw the line. There are no rules about when his prerogative no longer indicates caring but exploitation.

Although she accepts male-determined and -initiated contact, she does not fully anticipate its consequences. She is not a seer, and there are no crash courses on "Other-Womanhood," no reading list of "Old Other-Women's Tales." She may not have anticipated the acute and recurrent feeling of loneliness she has when their allotted time is over and he goes home to his wife:

> We would have a beautiful honeymoon and he would go home to his wife and kids. It was being as one but not being able to stay as one. Sharing him that much after our time together, I couldn't stand the pain. That was the worst thing about the relationship.

> I have more to lose. If things don't work out, I'm alone. He is still going home to someone. Whether things are good or bad, he is still going home to a situation, a routine, good or bad, it's still someone there. I'm alone and he's not. I cry a lot.

One of the major complaints of women who live alone, generally, is that they frequently feel alone—often enough, lonely. This is frequently seen as one of the major drawbacks of the single life. But because during the early stages of a relationship with a married man a woman somewhat escapes those lonely feelings, she can be taken unawares by the depth of her feeling of abandonment when, later in the relationship, she has grown closer to him. Unlike lovers who can think of parting as "such sweet sorrow," there is nothing sweet about separating from one's lover so he can return to another woman, his wife. Nor does the "morrow" necessarily bring her lover back to her. Indeed, his routine absence on particular "morrows"—such as weekends—affects her deeply. Unlike most of her peers, who she knows or believes are with their lovers on weekends, spending weekends in a conventional way, she is not. Since weekends come every week, she has a steady reminder that her time, her life, is controlled by an absent other:

> Sometimes he does shake some time loose on the weekends, and I want to be able to see him. So, I don't make too many weekend plans. Some weekends, its really the pits and I think I can't do this anymore. But I don't want to lose him. I love him.

> I remember one Sunday when he said he might call and come over and it rained all day. I just laid on the couch and watched television and got more and more depressed because he never called.

Unlike the fairly predictable routine engagements in regular relationships, the Other Woman's relationships are temporally erratic and intermittent. She has not anticipated the extent to which her lover's availability would control her own activities. She has not anticipated that being subject to changes in his plans on a day-to-day, week-to-week basis would cause her to alter her conventional routines so she could be available should he "shake some time loose," and she has not anticipated the feelings of powerlessness that arise from waiting and being cancelled.

This feeling of impotence derived from her inability to plan her own time is highlighted by its direct contrast with how she feels about holidays. From the beginning, the Other Woman anticipates that her lover will spend holidays with his family and that she will be on her own. She has prepared herself for that eventuality and she knows what to expect:

> His holidays are always with his family. I have other friends and stuff. I always had bunches of friends.

> I've never let him become the primary person in my life for holidays. I'm very close to my nieces and nephews and that's what I do. Spend the time with them.

Because she expects holidays to be difficult times, she can and does make plans for herself: Holidays are a kind of holiday *from* her married lover. Ironically, the most empowering gift he can give her is the guarantee he will not trespass on *her* free time.

To cancel engagements, arrive late, leave early, or simply not show up or phone indicates, generally, a lack of respect not only for the other person's time, but for them personally. For the Other Woman who is subject to this kind of neglect, something more than her time schedule and her ego are at stake: what is at stake is her fantasy of having found the ideal male-female relationship. Whether that ideal is some variant of chivalrous romantic love or of an egalitarian relationship or of some other storybook notion, most Other Women find that their fantasy, over time, fails them because the actual behavior of their married lover demonstrates the contrary. Neither her relationship nor herself commands his deepest respect.

Part of the reason he may not respect her is that she is the "other woman," a status that the culture stigmatizes and judges illicit, sinful, or neurotic. It would be difficult for any man to dissociate himself fully from those cultural stereotypes, despite his direct experience with his Other Woman. No matter how "good" a woman she is, no matter how intelligent, beautiful, kind, sexy, or empathic, her status as the "other woman" is a tainted one.[4] A woman who had traveled 700 miles to be with her married lover said:

> It was such a long drive going up there. Got there. He was a real prick about the whole thing. I really felt like the "other woman." I called him where he worked, and he set up a rendezvous. Back roads. I finally found the place and we went to a motel. We went to bed and all that kind of stuff, did some talking, and he went home. This was the Philadelphia area, and I thought I would stay in the city. He said, "Well, I don't want you on my doorstep." The way he said "you" was tinged with derision.

And part of the reason he may not totally respect her is that he may feel guilty about his own infidelity, and view the Other

Woman as the agent of his transgression. If he is troubled about his extramarital relationship and feels ashamed or fearful of having it discovered, he may act out those feelings by disregarding her needs and feelings. A woman who had shared a hotel room at a conference with her married lover said:

> I couldn't answer the phone when it rang, and he wouldn't hold my hand in the street. In the elevator, he would pretend he didn't know me. And then when he left, the last morning we got up and packed and a couple of his shirts had my make-up stains on them, white shirts, and he put them in the corner. I said, "You forgot your shirts." And he said, "No. I can't take them home with me." It made me feel a little soiled. He had put me in the role of the "other woman."

Another husband, whose wife suspected that he was having an affair, told the single woman he was involved with:

> I told my wife it wasn't you. I tried to protect your reputation.

In that particular situation and similar ones, the idea that her reputation needs protecting arises from his own uneasiness about having an extramarital relationship. Since these relationships are not socially legitimated and take place clandestinely, married men can see Other Women as "bad" and potentially dangerous. Because the man may believe he is a moral leper as well, he may alleviate his own guilt by labeling his lover the sinfully promiscuous one, as though casting stones at her will atone for his own transgressions.[5] If his aim is good, the woman's confusion and anguish can be great. Moreover, if he is successful in generating guilt in her, he may be reassured of her fidelity. Her bad times guarantee him good ones:

> He'd call me and accuse me of fucking around and that he knew it. I'd been at home reading books. I'd end up defend-

ing myself on the phone. I'd hang up and I felt so guilty I wondered why I hadn't gone around and fucked around. It was like, maybe I should have. Did I do it? Maybe I walked in my sleep. I got to the point where if I talked to another man, I felt guilty. It would be like, "Oh geez, I'm going to hear about this or I'm going to feel so guilty that I'll have to tell him."

Over a period of time, then, an Other Woman's sense of control over her life and time is diminished, her self-respect damaged. The conditions—secrecy, privacy, and time constraints—which had made her relationship seem special are now the very same ones that undermine her sense of worth, displace her energy, and dissipate her time. But other bad things can happen too: Other Women can be physically and psychologically abused by their married lovers *because* they are Other Women. Some men feel guilty toward their wives, and others have contempt for the "bad" woman they are involved with. Whichever, the underlying emotion can erupt in physical violence or in the psychological violence of being unfaithful to the Other Woman—of having other Other Women.

When men get physically violent, it is most likely to occur in relationships where women are psychologically and economically dependent.[6] A wife, for instance, stays in her marriage with an abusive husband because she is economically dependent upon him. She believes that she is bringing the abuse upon herself and that she somehow deserves it because he is so often so nice. Other Women who are economically and psychologically dependent on their married lovers may also be more likely to be abused, and may be more likely to remain in that abusive relationship.

A young executive's experience as a battered Other Woman is illustrative. She had been hired into a managerial position without the prerequisite education or experience. The married man who hired her, her supervisor, became her abusive lover:

In the beginning, I got a lot of stroking and self-esteem career-wise. He was a smoothie. A real winer-diner, very sophisticated, suave with his talking. The first three years were really upbeat. But, as I became more capable and attractive and lost weight, he became more insecure. Let's face it, he was still married. He didn't have as much to offer me as maybe somebody else.

During these early years, there was some physical abuse but "once only" was she "really terribly physically abused" by her "standards," when she "really got slapped around and held and bruised and those kinds of things." "Being beaten up and thrown and all that stuff" she attributed to stress based on his uncertainty about her commitment to him because he was married. Then he separated from his wife and the two moved into a new apartment together:

I thought things would be better because the stress would be off and he'd feel more secure about me. Everything would be really great and phenomenal and fantastic and then all of a sudden he'd say that I was this terrible person—not being sensitive to his needs. It could be about anything. About putting the toilet seat down. About answering the phone. Bingo, off the wall! Dr. Jekyll and Mr. Hyde.

Although not his wife, this young woman was economically dependent upon her abusing boss-lover. To break up with him would mean losing her job, which, in fact, she did. He fired her, and hired another single woman with whom he subsequently had a relationship. More insidious, she was trapped into the psychological dependency of seeing herself as the inept and insensitive one. He kept her, like a laboratory rat, on an erratic reward and punishment schedule—a schedule that encourages submissiveness in experimental animals and human beings. Like other battered women, she believed things would get better, that he was really a good man with an occasional aberration brought on by her own behavior, and that she needed him for survival.

Abuse of Other Women can take another form—his being involved with other Other Women. This is especially painful for the Other Woman because first and foremost she is a woman, and women see themselves as somehow the cause of a man's infidelity. They often believe that the male roams because the female is somehow inadequate.[7] If the man is having other relationships, the single woman's burgeoning self-esteem as an *attractive* woman, which was being confirmed by their relationship, gives way to insecurities. If the feelings of inadequacy grow, the relationship begins to feel more fragile, the Other Woman even less powerful, because she imagines rivals with whom she cannot compete.

Being displaced or betrayed creates considerable physical and emotional distress in women generally.[8] Yet, despite the intensity of a woman's feelings about being betrayed, unlike men, who are more likely to terminate such relationships and work to restore their self-esteem, women are likely to accept humiliation, swallow their pride, and proceed to work on fixing the damaged relationship. Other Women behave similarly. Even if an Other Woman should discover that she is not the second woman in his life but the third, fourth, or fifth, she may try to salvage the relationship:

> If it was just his wife he was not having such a hot time with, I would have felt better. But here was this other woman who had committed her life to him. And, here was another woman he was just starting up with.

> I finally learned why I was having so many vaginal infections. He was dipping into three or four different women!

> His friend told me that my lover had 12 women besides me on the line. When he came over that night, I told him what his friend had said fully expecting him to say, "He lies." Instead, he took out his large ring of keys. Picking them off one by one, he said, "This key gets me Jane, this key gets me Alice, this key gets me Deirdre," and on and on.

The distress and humiliation did not translate into action to terminate their relationships. Rather, they felt it was incumbent upon them to repair them. These women continued to see their married lovers, even though their feelings of self-worth and personal efficacy declined. The woman whose lover held all the keys, literally and metaphorically, eventually suffered a nervous breakdown as she tried, unsuccessfully, to please him, to accept his infidelities, to become Number One again.

Like any woman who has been betrayed, an Other Woman experiences intense pain and feelings of loss. But because she is an Other Woman, his betrayal is acute because she loses the illusion that her relationship is special and unique, her married lover wonderful. Now she wonders, "Have I become like his wife in his eyes? Is he talking about me to the Other Woman? How far does his deceit extend?"

Typically, women are more attuned to subtle nuances in relationships and more likely than men to feel jealous.[9] Once the potential for jealousy is set in motion for women, small infractions and perceived slights contribute to their suspicions. Everything he does or does not do can arouse suspicion:

There were other single women in the group [of work associates]. For all I know, he had something with all of us. There's no real proof. I still don't know one way or the other. It's one of those things you can't put your finger on.

He may have had three or four other girls on the string. I really believe that because once he got separated from his wife things got real weird. There was evidence of other women being around. It'd be like, "Well, I'm going to be real busy this weekend, so I can't see you," or "I've got an aunt coming in from out of town for Mother's Day." My gut said never to trust him. I should have trusted my gut. Weird phone calls. He always had an explanation, obviously, for everything.

But because jealousy is such a destructive emotion, single women, like married ones, may expend a great deal of energy denying reality. They would rather maintain the belief that their lover is faithful and that other factors explain his odd behavior or problems in the relationship. For example, his absence, fatigue, or "touchiness" can be attributed to the demands of his family or his work. But once his infidelity can no longer be denied, intense feelings of anger, pain, and fear erupt:

> I called him in Chicago when I wasn't supposed to. A woman answered. I was undone because I realized that this woman was more important to him than me. I was angry at myself for being so dumb. God, was I taken in. All the signs were there, but I didn't read them—didn't want to, I guess. Like him going on the weekends when his business was on Monday. Like not being allowed to call him there. Like him being too tired to make love when he came back. It felt like I was his wife. Like he was putting up with me. And cheating on me.

Another woman who had a relationship with her lover before he was married as well as during his marriage said:

> The night he got married, I really cracked up. I was a mess. But we kept seeing each other for five years more. Then his marriage was disintegrating, which was raising my hopes again. Well, I go out there for vacation like I always do, and at one point he props me in front of the fireplace and tells me he's going to get divorced and marry his old high school sweetheart. But he wants us to keep our relationship going! Incredible. I cried and cried.

Whatever ideals these women hold—that the relationship is special, that he is a knight in shining armor, that he will leave his wife—are decimated by his deceit. The single woman is not only *cheated on*, but *cheated of* her fantasy. This same man whom she has defined as a paragon of virtue, an honest man, has deceived her, just as he has deceived his wife:

It was the death of a dream.

Other dreams can die in these relationships as well, dreams about the kind of person one might be. Other Women can come to see their liaisons as an opportunity to accomplish other goals or to grow personally. For example, they may view their liaison as dovetailing with other agendas in their lives such as attaining educational or occupational goals. If they do not achieve their goals, they feel disappointed in themselves for they have failed to meet their own expectations. If the relationship does not turn out to fit conveniently into its compartment, if it does take more time and energy than she had imagined it would, the woman with other agendas may find that her sense of mastery and control—a part of her ideal image of herself—is damaged:

> Worst was the energy drain. The emotional drain, the being used up and tired. And the psychic energy that went into keeping the relationship at bay, and then to deal with the unexpected hurt. It ended up being very costly to me career-wise and life-wise.

This woman—and others like her—blames herself for poor judgment. She sees herself as having personally failed in using her relationship to achieve external goals, and she is disappointed in herself.

Other Women who view their liaison as an opportunity to experiment with acting differently with a man may also end up judging themselves harshly. If they do not break out of their old patterns with a married man, then they see themselves as personally deficient:

> I found it was the same pattern I had in the past with men. I was feeling put down. I felt I never quite measured up. I kept being afraid he'd think I was dumb, stupid, crude, uneducated, uncreative, or whatever.

Although the desire and opportunity were there for this woman to assert herself in a "safe" relationship, she fell back into her old patterns with men, seeing herself as less smart and less creative than they. Because in a relationship with a married man the opportunities for experimenting with and acting out different roles are so many, the potential for not measuring up to one's self-expectations is also great. Failing oneself in these liaisons is especially troublesome because women see them as a time and a place when they *should* be able to act differently. Old rationalizations for one's own inadequate behavior are difficult to sustain.

Because relationships between single women and married men provide immense opportunity for emotional intimacy, moreover, if a woman has had a history of emotional aloofness which she does not overcome in her liaison, she can come to see herself as incapable of ever being a loving, feeling person:

> These strong feelings were going on and I wasn't able to tell him. Loving is very precious. I have a hard time giving, and then when I wanted to, I couldn't. I hadn't changed. I was still troubled by emotional intimacy. Still resisted it.

> I've become what I most dislike in men—cold, calculating, unfeeling. I'm not sure I'll ever be able to be a really loving, giving person.

All the while, time goes on; the clock does not stop. Having the ideal relationship and being the ideal self is to have compensated, somehow, for the loss of actual time. If the barter works, if the fantasy can be played out and the woman can emerge from it empowered, pain and anger over the loss of time may be minimal. But if the actual relationship does not fulfill expectations and the ideal lover is in reality a common man, a flawed man, or a scoundrel, and the self she hoped to discover through the relationship eludes her, then anger and resentment can be overwhelming:

> I fantasize two different ways of killing him. One, I'd love to stand in front of him with a gun and point-blank shoot

him. Painfully, just shoot him. The other way I'd like to have him die is very slowly, and that's not a physical death. I'd like to ruin him credit-wise, reputation-wise, destroy his self-esteem. Ruin his life, like he ruined mine. He took everything. My youth. My dreams. You would think that someone who lives a life like he does, would die. Would be shot. I read the obits every day. Just to see. Just to see.

Most women's anger, pain, and humiliation is less extreme, but few escape feelings of having lost time and of being disappointed in themselves and their lovers. The married man's time schedule determined hers. By controlling her time, he came to control much of her life, an outcome she had not bargained on. Because she is in the stigmatized role of the "other woman," at any time she can be disregarded, put down, or even abused by her married lover. When the relationship falls short of her hopes, as it almost invariably does, she feels disillusioned. And because she may not be able to act out the person she wants to be in the relationship, she is disappointed in herself as well.

All these different losses—time, self-esteem, and dreams—depress and disempower women. In a particularly insidious way, though, the fact that a woman feels badly in the relationship may serve to keep her in it. When people, generally, lose feelings of self-esteem and self-determination, it is difficult for them to *act*. They accept ill-treatment as their due because they believe they deserve it and cannot imagine better alternatives. When it is a woman who has lost self-esteem in a relationship, she tries to repair it. The greater her dependence on the relationship, the more likely she is to try to rectify it rather than leave it.[10] In consequence, the very women who are losing the most by being in their relationships—time, ego, dreams—are the ones least able to extricate themselves: The more time she has invested, the more difficult it is for her to get out. But not only do all good things come to end, so do all bad things.

Chapter Eight

ENDINGS

Gᴇᴏʀɢᴇ Sɪᴍᴍᴇʟ noted that a dyad, the group with only two members, is the most fragile of human relationships because if one person leaves, the relationship dies.[1] In a dyad, you are always at the mercy of the other.

Relationships between single women and married men are dyads. And although they can and do last for years and decades, they usually do end. Mostly, the husbands stay with their wives. A few single woman–married man relationships are transformed into marriages, but proportionally only a few. Although men who divorce often have had an extramarital relationship, the overwhelming majority of men who leave their wives "for" the Other Woman do not end up marrying her. They marry someone else.[2]

The single woman has played a role in his marriage by providing a therapeutic outlet for his grievances and fantasies. In all likelihood, the Other Woman has underestimated the power of his wife, family, and children, because she has denied their existence or has believed that her lover was in a "bad marriage." But his wife comes out of the shadows. If she comes out fighting she is more likely to keep her marriage, for she has the weight of the institution of marriage and their shared history, children, and property on her side.[3] Despite the increasing accessibility of divorce, the economic and social costs for women who divorce are very high. This, combined with women's willingness to work on their relationships, causes many wives to resist giving up their marriages.[4] And because the emotional and financial costs of divorce for men are high, particularly the loss of regular contact with their children, wives are often successful in pulling their husbands back into the family and even into the marriage.[5]

Some men leave their wives when they are going through a midlife crisis. Work, family, aging, and death are unresolved issues for them. Their whole lives may feel in limbo, uncertain, and unfulfilling.[6] If the single woman's married lover is going through a tumultuous midlife passage, she may serve as a tunnel, but not the light at the end. She becomes, in effect, an integral part of his marriage and his midlife passage, and should he no longer need his wife or should he resolve his crisis, he no longer needs the Other Woman either:

I was the breakthrough for him, for dealing with what was going on in his life.

I don't want to be the bridge out for another married man.

People often unwittingly choose the lovers they do because those lovers can help them achieve other goals. It is not simply that one is attracted sexually to the lover, but that that person will be "useful." Once their usefulness is over, the relationship wanes. The married man, for example, may choose an Other Woman who facilitates his departure from the marriage, a woman who represents youth and excitement. If he feels young again, it proves that his hidden goals are not impossible to obtain. But once the marriage is over, he is ready to find a different relationship, one that does not remind him of his previous marriage and his feelings of aging. Young, intelligent, and accomplished single women, on their part, may also be using the married man for reasons other than love and sex. He may serve as a way station, or mentor, or nondemanding "friend" while she works on her identity, builds a career, or raises a family. If he should leave his wife, the Other

Woman may leave him because the advantages of a "safe" relationship are now lost.

If the separated husband and the single woman begin acting like a "regular" couple, new problems may emerge. Because the relationship has been constructed in private, both partners may have a rude awakening when they present their relationship to friends and families and find they are uncomfortable in each other's social network. They may also find that annoyances which seemed trivial when the relationship was perceived as temporary take on greater significance. Negotiating mundane, everyday life can reduce the aura of romance.

But perhaps the most emotionally cogent reason against the Other Woman and the ex-married man getting married is that, because their relationship was a duplicitous one, neither can wholly trust the other's claims of future fidelity:

> I'd never marry a married man that cheated on his wife. I think that is crazy.

> I don't see how people can get married to each other when they have a history of multiple relationships. There is a tremendous amount of emotional and financial commitment in a marriage and unless you know he'll be true blue, I certainly wouldn't bother getting married.

People, generally, who have been unfaithful are the most likely to suspect their partners of infidelities.[7] Distrust and jealousy arise simultaneously, creating paranoia about the stability of the relationship and undermining the basis for love as well as the impetus for marriage. It is painful to discover one's partner is unfaithful, but "stupid to let yourself in for it" when your partner-to-be is a "known adulterer":

> Don't think he's going to leave his wife and kids and come make you a swell husband, 'cause you're going to be the one he runs around *on* instead of the one he runs around with.

Relationships between single women and married men are grounded in secrecy, deceit, and betrayal. No matter how loving and caring the relationship may appear to the single woman, the reality is that her relationship with a married man is based upon his infidelity. Another woman, his wife, is being deceived. If the single woman should become his new wife, their history as a history of partners in deceit will be hard to put to rest and to forget.

Because there are many obstacles to husbands leaving their wives for Other Women, and many more to Other Women and married men becoming a married couple, relationships between single women and married men generally end without being transformed into marriages. As in most personal relationships, liaisons end because one partner, or the other, or both have lost interest in maintaining the relationship—the costs exceed the benefits.[8] But how the ending is accomplished—why it ends, who rejects whom, and how long it takes—has consequences for one's feelings about oneself and the future.

In any male-female relationship, the male can reject the female, the female reject the male, or both of them can mutually reject the relationship. In terms of one's positive feelings about oneself, the old bromide that it is better to give than to receive is true: It is far better to give notice that the relationship is over than it is to be served with that notice. It is far better to be in control of one's life, one's time, and one's destiny than to have it determined by another. But for most women, emotionally, it is probably even better if the relationship ends by mutual agreement with neither party rejecting the other.[9]

Whether one determines how and when a relationship ends is highly correlated with how much power one has had in the relationship. Between single women and married men, as we have seen, women can be quite dependent. Unwittingly, perhaps, many Other Women are passive and wait for their lovers' call, visit, or action. Dependency can become so great that they cut themselves off from their co-workers, friends, and family. The married man can become her whole life, a life in which she loses her self-esteem and feelings of personal efficacy. But not all Other Women act in this way. There are some women who remain fairly independent in their relationships. These are women who tend to be strongly

committed to goals other than marriage and who act more asser-
tively. As might be expected, the more dependent a woman is in
her relationship, the less likely she is to end it and the more likely
she is to suffer pain and humiliation during the ending phase.
Women who are more assertive are more likely to do the rejecting
or be part of a mutually agreed upon ending, and are less likely
to be grief-stricken when the liaison terminates.

Married men may end their liaisons because of their wives,
their careers, or their new lovers. His wife may give him an ultima-
tum, and he may reevaluate the importance of his wife and family.
Career advancement may require him to leave the liaison or the
city, or he may have begun a new extramarital relationship. When
women remain quite independent in their relationships, these same
external factors may play a role but with a twist. If he leaves his
wife, the Other Woman may terminate the relationship; *her* occupational mobility may exclude a continued liaison with him; or she
may have found herself a new lover.

Internal stresses, or problems arising from within the relationship, may also create a breach. The disjunction between the expectations and the reality becomes too great to sustain the myth about
the relationship, or one (or both) of the parties outgrow their need
for the relationship:

I always told myself when things got bad enough I'd get
out. They finally got bad enough.

He told me that what I needed him for today, I wouldn't
need him for tomorrow. He was right.

The interplay of internal and external factors can reach crisis
proportions, especially for women who are highly dependent upon
their married lovers. Because of his wife's demands—an external
factor—he may not be available when the Other Woman's needs
are greatest—an internal stress. One woman's account of her grief
over her father' death, another's jealousy of her sister's wedding,
and a third's abortion trauma are illustrative:

When my father died, I was so alone. He [married lover] had to go to a picnic—a *picnic.* Hers. He said he couldn't get out of it. Her picnic versus me. I hated him then. Nothing was ever right after that.

Here I was turning 30. Seven years of my life gone and my little sister was getting married and I felt—I wanted so desperately to be a wife. His wife. God, anybody's wife. I began to feel ashamed and useless and used. Damn it. *Used.*

I had to go and get some character in a slimy room and pay bunches of hundred dollars. And I hated him because I had the abortion. Because I had thought that if he could have married me, I wouldn't have had to have the abortion. So I blamed him.

Life's major passages—deaths, weddings, pregnancies—are especially destabilizing for the Other Woman because they cannot be processed in a socially normal way. She is alone, and more intensely so than she would be if she had no relationship at all, because there is the hope, the hidden expectation, that he will "be there" for her in major crises at least:

I was fooling myself. I thought he could be depended upon for the big things—that he would be there if I really needed him. He wasn't.

On the other hand, for women who have been more independent in their relationships, internal stresses are more likely to arise if the male escalates his demands upon her. One woman who had chosen a married man because she wanted an emotionally cool relationship commented:

I'm not a very warm person. I never wanted to be somebody's mother. I began to see him as weak—draining me. I had my work to do. I wanted to do my work.

Another woman who was bisexual and had enjoyed her relationship with a married man because there were few demands on her said:

> He was going to tell his wife that night. I freaked. I panicked.
> I told him not to. I loved him, but suddenly I saw white
> picket fences and the P.T.A. If I married him—if I married
> anyone—I would lose my lifestyle. I didn't want to be a
> wife. I began to realize that I was going to be a lesbian
> not because I'm not attracted to men—I still am—but because
> I didn't want to risk losing the women's community. He
> was asking me to give up too much.

For women who are more assertive in, and less committed to, their relationships, his escalating expectations cause them to reassess the place of the relationship in their lives; if the relationship cannot be de-escalated, the woman may decide to end it.

Deciding that a relationship is going to end, however, is not the same as accomplishing it. Action on the part of one or both of the partners is required. As in other personal relationships, there are different sequences or timetables by which the ending is accomplished: the precipitate, quick *shock-out;* the long-drawn-out, on-again and off-again *drag-out;* and the slow petering out until the relationship ends, or the *wind-down.*

Sometimes women who are fairly independent in their relationships initiate the shock-out. One woman who had found a new lover wrote her old one a "Dear John" letter. She recounted:

> I delayed a long time writing. I didn't want to hurt him.
> He had such a fantasy about me, and about us, seven years
> up the road. I finally decided the only way out was the
> direct and clean one, so I wrote him a simple good-bye letter.
> He wrote wishing me luck and told me to keep his address
> just in case. I didn't.

Or in another case, a woman's career advancement hastened the ending:

> I had received my promotion and was going to national head-
> quarters within the month and I was so excited I just blurted
> it out on the phone. He was silent for a long time and then
> said, "What about me? Us?" I wanted to laugh, and I was
> furious too. No congrats or anything. Then I felt sorry for
> him. I guess it came as a shock to him. I was really going.

These women almost invariably see their decision quickly to
end their liaison as unalterable and inviolate. One woman throws
away her ex-lover's address; another does not alter her career plans.
The relationship with the married man has served its purpose,
and it is time for it to be over. As a woman, socialized into considering another's feelings, she is attuned to his feelings of loss and
may even feel guilty, but she does not alter her plans because he
feels rejected or has an "irrational outrage at being deserted."

Men, though, are more likely to be use the shock-out. Because
men are less skilled in tending to another's feelings,[10] and because
they may not realize their centrality in the Other Women's life,
Other Women can be left in a "heartless and inconsiderate" manner. Occasionally, that may mean she is left for another Other
Woman:

> I was going into the hospital to have my tubes tied so I
> wouldn't get pregnant and confuse things between us. He
> was supposed to come into town to bring me. He didn't
> show up, so I drove myself. I didn't ever hear from him
> again. Later I learned that he had fallen in love with someone
> else and had left his wife for her.

Probably more commonly, though, she is abandoned because
of his career considerations. For example, one man received a major
career promotion and chose summarily to leave behind all vestiges
and reminders of his lower status, including his Other Woman:

> I dreamed that when his promotion came he would be finan-
> cially able to leave his wife. When it came through, he told

me we would have to stop seeing each other. That his position made him too public, too visible, too vulnerable. Just like that. Three years. Poof. Over.

Another Other Woman, who was a research assistant, learned through an office memo that her lover/boss was moving to another city with the entire project staff except her. She lost her relationship and her job, and acquired no reasonable explanation for either:

After I read the memo, I stood shocked. Only the week before, for a period of nearly one day, I thought it might turn into something permanent. He never told me personally that I wasn't moving with the staff. To this day, I don't know exactly why I was left behind. Why he did it that way.

And yet another, who had twice changed jobs and twice moved across country to be near her married lover, simply received a postcard from him that said:

I am moving to Korea. Due to a lack of propinquity, I shall be removed without a chance to totally resolve our relationship. Have a good life. [Unsigned].

These women, and others like them, have abruptly lost their married lover, and they have been treated as though their relationship held little value or meaning to him and no explanation is necessary. Because he ends the relationship precipitately, though, she is deprived of closure—of the right to say good-bye. Women who were highly committed to the relationship may, therefore, refuse to give up hope and may refuse to accept that the relationship is over. For example, four years after receiving the postcard from Korea, that Other Woman said:

If he came through this door right now I'd want to say, "Who the hell are you coming in and out of my life whenever you want?" but I'm afraid I know I would just say, "Hi! Okay, coffee?"

Deprived of final closure, the dependent Other Woman continues to hold onto the hope that he will return. If she lacks a familial or social support network, as this Other Woman did, she may have to seek psychotherapy, which this woman has, in order to get some distance on her relationship. But even then she is likely to carry with her for a long while unresolved feelings of abandonment and loss.

Equally difficult, although less common, is having one's lover die. The Other Woman is deprived of saying good-bye to him as well as of the usual rituals we have for working through grief— the emotional and physical presence of friends and relatives, the funeral, the socially legitimated identity of mourner:

> He died of a heart attack. Very suddenly. It was really hard because there was no closure and I didn't go to his funeral and I still think at some level I haven't accepted that he is dead. I can still walk down the street and see a man from the back and I'll think it's him, and then I realize he is dead.

When people grieve, they search for their loved one in crowds and on the street. This is a typical bereavement reaction.[11] These strong reactions to his loss—enshrinement, denying he is dead, looking for him—are indicators of the intensity of the bond the Other Woman felt toward her married lover. Without the support of friends, family, and community to share and work through her bereavement, she can carry that grief with her for many years.

His wife's discovering or suspecting his extramarital relationship can precipitate a rapid end of his affair also. Although the single woman may enter the relationship believing that his wife and marriage will have priority, she probably does not expect to be simply "dumped." One woman, who normally communicated with her lover through their computer network, returned home after spending a week with him at a convention. She recounted:

I'd send him messages on-line [through the computer net-work] and he wouldn't respond. He'd barely talk [on-line]. I was beside myself. I think his wife must have intuited it [the relationship]. And there was no way to find out. I need a chance to sit with him in a bar, where we're not too alone, and have him tell me the truth about why it's over. I want it resolved.

A sudden ending foisted on the single woman, because of an-other woman, his work mobility, his death, or his wife, leaves the Other Woman without an opportunity to achieve closure. If the relationship has been shrouded in secrecy, friends will not be able to provide much insight on what specifically went awry, and they may give her scant emotional support. If she cannot talk to her married lover about why the relationship has ended, or cannot trust his explanation, a satisfactory emotional resolution will continue to elude her. Since the women most likely to be summarily discarded are the women who are more passive in their relationships, they have fewer internal resources to rebuild their self-esteem. Not achieving closure may slow down or abort per-sonal growth and create new problems with men. Predictably, then, women who have been less powerful in their relationships with married men and who have been abandoned by them are those most likely to have problems in their subsequent relationships with men:

If I do meet somebody, I immediately retreat out of fear of rejection. I don't know if that is a temporary or absolutely permanent condition.

After him, I went through my wild stage. I started dating and sleeping with just anybody. Not very discerning at all.

I hate men.

I guess I haven't accepted that it is really over. I don't want to move or anything in case he does try to find me.

Although various amounts of time have passed since the relationship has ended, each of these women is still being affected by the man's behavior in various ways: fear of new relationships, brief encounters, impersonal sex, low expectations, hostility toward men, and waiting for him to return. In direct contrast, highly independent women who initiated the sudden ending are more likely to find subsequent relationships more satisfactory:

I started dating "available" men, and within a year I was living with a printmaker. We're getting married soon.

The fellow I am seeing seriously now introduces me to all his friends and takes me everywhere.

Men are my friends. I don't want a lover now, but I enjoy my single men friends.

Whether it is marriage, a serious relationship, or friendship that these women subsequently seek, they continue to be assertive about their preferences in relationships.

Not all relationships end precipitately. Some *drag out* and drag on over a period of months or years; sometimes, it takes longer to end the relationship than it did to construct it. On-again, off-again, on-again: in such endings, the ambivalence of one partner and the desire of the other mesh and criss-cross, keeping them both entangled.

Characteristically, during drag-outs the single woman believes that her lover will leave his wife or that he will reform. The more time she has invested in believing her construction of reality and the more time she has spent on the emotional seesaw, the harder it becomes for her to withdraw.[12] The law of negative sacrifice takes hold: Having put in this much time and emotion, she reasons, she might as well invest some more. This justifies the losses already accrued—like sending in more soldiers to justify the death of the first platoon.

Even fairly assertive women sometimes find themselves engaged in a drag-out ending. One woman, a feminist and an executive, who did not wish to marry her married lover, was nevertheless embroiled in a long drag-out because she kept believing he could change:

> I would break up with him every January for years. I would grieve all spring. By July everyone would say how good I looked. I would just be getting over him and we'd get together again. Each time I thought he had finally understood my needs for independence, and each time I have been wrong.

Another woman, a student involved with a professor, was similarly embroiled:

> It was back and forth like a Ping-Pong ball. Each time we got back together, our relationship had deteriorated more. I started looking for someone else. I didn't close doors to other opportunities. I finally got out.

In both of these situations, the women struggled to free themselves from a relationship which was squandering their time and energy. In the process of terminating the relationship, they were open to other options. Although getting out dragged on, it did not totally debilitate them because they felt some sense of power over their lives. They could imagine a life without their married man.

Some Other Women cannot imagine a life without their lover. No matter how painful that relationship is, it is viewed as preferable to losing him. For example, one woman who had been physically abused by her lover and who had gone through two years of intensive therapy while the relationship's ending dragged out said:

> I can't give up loving him, but I can give up the idea of living with him.

For this woman, and others like her, traditional femininity—passivity and dependency—have been so hyperextended that she has great difficulty acting in her own best interest. Other Women like her may so submerge their identities that they think of themselves not as people, but as malleable objects:

> I told him I would be anything he wanted me to be. *Anything.*

Women who are willing to be defined by their lovers, to become whatever the man wants them to be, often find themselves involved in interminably long and painful endings. Some of these highly dependent women believe their lover will eventually leave his wife. Even if he does not, they are willing to "accept whatever he does."

Some fairly autonomous women also believe he will leave his wife because he says he is going to. If she wishes to marry him or live with him or even have a more normal relationship, then, his verbal commitment keeps her on the relationship seesaw:

> He said, "I can't leave just yet. It would hurt her too much." I said, "How long?" He said, "About a month." A month went by and, obviously, he wasn't going to leave her. We met and I think I ended it. It all blurs, because he came back. That was the pattern. He'd come back and say he was working on it. I still believed him. I believed him and I loved him. Back and forth. Back and forth.

> When I met him, I asked was he divorced or married. He lied. He kept lying. It was six months before I finally figured out this guy was not even separated. For three and a half years he kept telling me he was working on the divorce. He was doing nothing.

Sometimes her belief that "he'll leave his wife" is supported by his actions. One husband left his wife—and returned to her—three times during the final year of his extramarital liaison:

> Each time he left her, I thought it was for good. Each time he had some reason to go back—her fake suicide, helping

her open the summer house. She fought for him. She wouldn't let him go. I couldn't let him go either. She was very persistent. Very flattering to him. Finally, he said, "I just can't go on. She's won. She's beaten me down."

If the single woman grows fond of her married lover—fond enough to want a more normal relationship—she may want him to leave his wife, and may raise that issue with him herself. By doing so, she is attempting to assert herself and her needs in the relationship. However, a request that he leave his wife may tip the delicate balance that has kept the relationship free from conflict. One fairly independent woman told her married lover to "choose." He said he "would be darn lucky to have her and would work toward that goal." From then on, "everything was thrown into a tizzy":

He would just flip back and forth, promising me everything and looking like he was going to do everything, to saying, "I can't see you anymore." And every time he would do that, I would be devastated. There were months of this. Up and down. Up and down. He'd say, "Okay, now I've done it," and the next thing I knew he'd tell me he and his wife were going on a vacation to Phoenix. When he came back, he gave me a framed oil painting and crab lice!

During this yearlong "emotional roller coaster" ride, her lover moved with his wife and children to another city, enrolled in a graduate program, left his wife but went into marriage counseling with her, and agreed not to see the Other Woman any longer. In fact, he was seeing her so often that he had a morning paper delivered to her house in his name, and he had life insurance policies taken out for her sons. Despite how strongly his life had become merged with the Other Woman's and despite all the indicators that he intended them to have a future together, he could not, finally, separate himself from his marriage, wife, and children. After a passel of "false promises, lost sleep, and broken expectations," the Other Woman began to feel both "anesthetized and angry":

It became obvious to me that his marriage was not going to end, and each abrupt swing still hurt. But I got angrier each time. After four of his "I can't see you again—I am leaving her now" fluctuations compressed into two weeks, I finally told him I didn't want to see him anymore. He called and called and called, but I refused to talk to him. I tore up his letters unopened and returned his presents.

Nearly a year later, he contacted her again. He told her that he and his wife had gone through a "recommitment ceremony" and that their new marriage contract included his right to see her. She told him she "wasn't interested." Two years after she ended the relationship, she remarried:

I invited him and his wife to my wedding. Almost spitefully. They came. She certainly didn't look very happy, but I can imagine she decided they were going. She still asks him about our relationship and what we did and where we went. He says he lies to her about it.

Although this relationship is ostensibly over, the emotional aftermath is not totally buried. Drag-outs are emotionally exhausting, even for fairly independent women, and extraordinarily time-consuming. Enmeshed in an on-again, off-again relationship, the woman lacks clarity as to when the relationship is really over. The social context warps the messages that are sent, hindering her interpretation. Yet if its history has been to start up again, and if one has already "gone through so much together," why stop now? The law of negative sacrifice takes a stranglehold now. After months and sometimes years of limbo, women are exhausted:

I wish he had died. If he died while I was still loving him, I would have been in mourning, but it sure would have been a lot easier to have picked up the pieces. I would have been three years recovered by now.

I survived.

May it [the relationship] rest in peace.

Least traumatic of endings are those that *wind down* slowly through a steady process of decelerating involvement. Like a spinning top, a wind-down relationship slows down gradually until it eventually topples over from lack of momentum. Sometimes the wind-down is so slow and gradual that women who are highly dependent and submissive may not recognize that the relationship has, for all practical purposes, withered and died. If they refrain from acknowledging the reality, they can hope that it is not really over, that there is still a chance. Although being uncertain about the status of the relationship is painful, it is not as emotionally costly as being abandoned or involved in a long drag-out:

> He moved to start a new job and I got there once and we stayed together, but it just started to founder. I was kind of hurt, really hurt. I thought he would call and this and that. I called him a couple times, but he wouldn't talk. So basically we have lost touch. But I realized that we didn't ever really talk about it and that he wouldn't.

The more independent the woman is in her relationship, the more credit she takes for its slow demise. Such women see the ending as the logical outcome of a series of choices they have made, because each choice distances them from the relationship:

> I found myself choosing to be alone or with clients or working on a competition. I found myself looking forward more to the times apart, rather than to the times together. The times between seeing each other grew longer, and the time spent together shorter. The better I became as an architect, the less need I had to be with him.

> Ending it was like being on a train pulling into a station. You know well before the city limits, it is going to stop and you're going to get off. You spend the last of the trip

preparing to leave. There's something bittersweet about trips, don't you think?

In wind-down endings where women feel they have been in charge, bitterness, a sense of unfinished business, or guilt about abandoning their lovers is virtually absent. Their energies have not been diverted into an emotionally exhausting brouhaha, and they are ready to move on to the next phase of their life. When the wind-down is a mutual decision, ending the liaison may be a relief:

It just waned. The last time I was going to be with him and felt I had to use the vibrator before he showed up because the sex was so bad, I thought this is the last time. And then he never showed up, anyway.

We saw each other less and less. My other relationship was beginning to be more important. Then he said his marriage counselor told him he should stop seeing me if he wanted his marriage to work. He made it easy for me, and I said, "If that's what you want, then that's it."

I was finishing school, he was moving, and my old boyfriend had returned to town. I was just kind of wrapping things up. Ready to get on with the next stage of my life.

In each of these situations, the Other Woman no longer valued the relationship. Nor, apparently, did her married lover. Without really planning to end the relationship, time, change, or new relationships converged to terminate it. These fairly lackadaisical mutual endings, though, are probably not as liberating as those when both partners *purposefully* find a time and a way to end the liaison so that the single woman leaves feeling whole and empowered. If a relationship can end with both parties taking equal responsibility for its completion and with both parties feeling that the time is right to end it, then bitterness, or resentment, or lack of closure do not pursue her. There are no guarantees, of course, that the Other Woman and her married man can achieve this, because there are imponderables beyond their control, such as ill health, death, or his wife. But they can try to decide together how and when the relationship, as a lover-to-lover relationship, will end:

> We knew from the beginning that it would have to end. We didn't really want it to end, but it was appropriate that it should. So it was a matter of finding a suitable time. I saw him being very careful about this, so that I wouldn't be damaged by it, just as he was being careful that his wife wouldn't be damaged.

After several "false" endings, this woman's career took her to a city 700 miles away. They discussed her moving as another "opportunity" for ending. She continued to see her lover, although less frequently and less intensely, for a while thereafter. Now the sexual and romantic liaison is over, but they continue to communicate by letter and phone:

> It has become nostalgic and comfortable. It hasn't finished because I still have warm feelings for him, still feel there's things I want to tell him about.

This woman, and others like her, feel comfortable with their feelings about their ex-lovers; they think of them warmly, as friends. The relationship has come full circle—they are friends *again* as they were before they were lovers, but now the circle is deeply etched:

> People imprint on you, and that part of you which they imprinted, which you shared, or which became important to you because of that person will always belong to that person. You'll always be connected to that person.

The importance of being friends with ex-lovers is a recurrent theme among women. Frequently, even those who have "gone

through hell" with their married lovers and those who were abandoned wish to have the married man as their friend *again:*

> I want to be friends with him. To be able to talk. I enjoyed
> him so much. I'd love to call him for lunch or a drink. I've
> managed to maintain friendships with a number of single
> men I used to date. This has been extremely important to
> me. A source of pride.

> If I chose well enough to get involved in the first place,
> then the least I can do is to maintain the friendship.

Friendship is where many of these relationships started. The
single woman was flattered by his interest, helped by his knowledge, and drawn to his person. She sincerely believed that they
were friends, and friendship for women implies longevity and loyalty. If the single woman can regain that friendship, she can feel
that he is worthy, after all, that her judgment is not totally faulty;
she loved well, if not wisely.

That women want to believe that friendship with ex-lovers is
desirable, even when the man has treated them poorly, is a testimony to the power of social imperatives in defining women's feelings. Indeed, the desire of women to be friends with men both
before and *after* the love relationship may very well be one of the
major ways in which women's sexuality is socially controlled and
ultimately constrained. Women, as we have seen, associate friendship with sex and love. As a friend who is sexually attracted to
a man, feelings of love seem to be a natural outcome. Because
men do not have these same definitions and associations, though,
when women become friends with men they are at a disadvantage.
Women's expectations of themselves as friends are to be accepting
and understanding, caring and intimate. To lose a friend, for
women, is a major loss because it signifies to themselves that they
have experienced interpersonal failure: They have chosen poorly
or they have erred, somehow, in the management of their friendship. If a woman believes that being friends is the best way to
finish a relationship, she may find herself swallowing his version

of the truth, repressing anger and resentment, avoiding conflict, and contorting her feelings and definitions of the situation to mesh with his, all in the name of her idea of friendship:

> He's still somebody very important to me. Very. Why am I saying this? I'm hearing myself saying it, and I can't believe I'm saying it. Is this an old tape that he should be important to me? That I should care about him? Maybe it's my need to care rather than his calling that out in me.

And so in the endings, the relationships come full circle. Many end as they began—in a friendship or the need to believe that there is a friendship. Most salient, the ending is consistent with how the relationship was begun and carried out. Women who have been more powerful in their relationships tend to remain empowered, whereas women who have submerged their identities become even more powerless. For some women, especially highly submissive ones, the pain of the ending is intense, the emotional fallout terrifying. For others, ending the relationship is empowering. Whether the relationship ends because of changes in jobs, his death, another woman, issues with his wife, or internal problems within the relationship is less crucial, for the woman's well-being, than who initiates the action: It is always better for her to be the rejecting lover rather than the rejected. But it is even better for her if the relationship can end through mutual and agreeable consent. Because women have been socialized as women, though, and want to be considerate and to repair relationships if at all possible, and because the norms that govern male-female relationships disadvantage women, frequently the Other Woman invests more than she had intended in her relationship and more than her married lover. Because of these factors, most Other Women—despite their seeming liberation and autonomy in the workplace and with friends—do not control the endings of their liaisons.

Relationships between single women and married men sometimes end quickly, sometimes drag out, and sometimes wind down slowly. They generally do end. But new ones start: For better or worse, single women continue to get involved with married men.

Chapter Nine

THE FUTURE OF THE OTHER WOMAN

Being the Other Woman appears to be a viable solution for legions of contemporary single women. Many of these women believe their emotional involvement will be limited and their relationships will dovetail with the pursuit of other goals. Sensing the potential for greater independence and autonomy in their liaison, they imagine they will be in control of themselves and the relationship. But what mostly happens to these "new" Other Women is what happened to previous generations of Other Women. They lose control and their relationship ends up benefiting the man more than the woman: Being a new Other Woman has the same old consequences.

Few of the 33 million never-married, divorced, and widowed women in America today[1] expect they will spend large portions of their lives as single women. Yet many of them will. For any woman over the age of 25, there is a serious shortage of men; a single woman over 35 will probably be single for the rest of her life.[2] Even fewer single women, though, plan on having a long-term relationship with a married man. Yet many of them do have such a relationship. All kinds of single women from all social strata—regular, normal, everyday, women—get involved with married men. Some stay in these relationships for years.

There is little doubt that liaisons between single women and married men will continue to be common in the future because the demographic and social factors which have encouraged them will not disappear: Fewer and fewer men will be available for women now older than 25; the expectation that women be heterosexually involved will not expire; the sexually permissive culture will not dissipate; changing aspirations and increased options for women in the wake of the women's movement will not be eradicated; and women's need for time while they pursue goals other than getting married will not cease.

Because these relationships will continue to be a significant social phenomenon, it is important to assess them and to question their implications for the future. The best place to begin is to ask how the Other Woman evaluates these relationships in terms of her own future. Would she herself have another relationship with a married man?

Some women have needs that make another liaison with a married man appear to be a reasonable option, whatever its drawbacks. For older, divorced women who have lived most of their lives financially dependent on men and who have limited earning capacity and little ability to compete in the singles' market, such a liaison may serve as an economic resource. A married man can provide some financial benefits that she cannot provide for herself. Similarly, women who are beginning graduate school or low-paying apprenticeships, and who cannot find a single man or do not wish to be involved with an available man, may welcome the extras a married man may provide, such as vacations or dinners.

Other women may want relationships which are cool and emotionally distant, while they pursue career or educational goals, or they may want a relationship that provides sex without undue commitment to or time demands from their lover. These are styles of relating Other Women see as more obtainable with a married man, although, as we have seen, even the coolest of contemporary women often find themselves having their time controlled and their energy depleted by their married lovers. Being able to isolate and control their emotions is not a guaranteed outcome; Other Woman may find themselves more dependent in their liaisons than they had planned on.

In addition to women's needs for either economic support or

emotionally distant relationships, some women are seeking egalitarian relationships, and believe they are more likely to find those with married men:

> I have a very clear picture of how I want a relationship to be with a man. In these [single woman–married man] relationships, it's closer to my ideal than others. Maybe it's because you don't have to fight about things, picky things, and turf isn't an issue. You're really on the same side. And isn't that what we want in a relationship with a man anyway? To have some time when the man isn't the enemy. And he isn't the enemy because he doesn't have to assert his ownership. Because he owns somebody else, he doesn't have to own you.

Finding emotional equity with a man is difficult because men fear emotional vulnerability and expect male dominance and female dependency in intimate relationships.[3] If a woman believes she has found an equal relationship with a married man, then she may seek such a relationship again, preferring it, whatever its problems might be, to those found in a "regular" male-privileged one. She attributes its seeming equity to his marital status and expects future liaisons to be similarly positive. What she may not be recognizing is that this relationship appears more egalitarian because there is less chance for conflict over the day-to-day management of a home and budget, not to mention the power struggles over career precedence, the having and rearing of children, and economic priorities. What appears to her as an egalitarian relationship is, in actuality, an untested one.[4]

In contrast to those women who would get involved again with a married man, some Other Women are ambivalent about such liaisons. Their ambivalence stems from an uncertainty about themselves as people and about what they want in future relationships, an uncertainty which has been exaggerated by their experience with a married man. Unable to proceed with their own self-defined agendas because they lack confidence in themselves, they place themselves "on hold." The more fragile their ego, the greater a

man's power to shape and direct them, a shaping many women
wish to resist. But when a woman's self-esteem is low, a man's
attentions are comforting. Consequently, Other Women who lack
a firm sense of self are ambivalent about involvements generally
and about more permanent ones in particular:

> I don't want anything to be named. I don't want to make
> distinctions between friends and lovers. I don't want to make
> commitments and close off other options.

> I don't want to make a decision on whether or not to get
> married again, so basically a married man is safe. I'm not
> sure what I want or what I'm looking for.

Being with a married man keeps one out of circulation, while
the search for self-knowledge, self-esteem, and awareness continues. A relationship with a married man might buy time to find
oneself and to establish one's direction. But if a woman comes
out of her relationship without a deeper understanding of self or
of her expectations from a relationship, what guarantees are there
that the consequences of a new liaison will be any different? One's
life can be spent avoiding basic issues: Who am I? Should I marry
or not marry?

> When I was 23, it was romantic to be in love with a married
> man. At 25 there was still this element of romanticism and
> sophistication. You get to 38 and you find out it's not sophis-
> ticated. I can't say I've wasted my life, because I've been
> looking.

Many single women, though, strongly reject the idea of ever
again being the Other Woman. The painful feelings associated with
their relationship have so changed them that being an Other
Woman has no future place in their lives. These women attribute
the problems in their relationships directly to the fact that their
lover was married. In future relationships, they want to avoid married men:

It has forever cured me of the notion that I could either live with or approve of a nonmonogamous situation. Absolutely, I can't take it. Too much denial. Too much repression. Too much pitying yourself.

Now I want clean-cut relationships. I don't want to get involved with people who are attached to other people because it hurts! It's very confusing and I end up feeling I give more than I get. It just doesn't feel good. I don't like feeling I'm in competition with another woman. What I want now is exclusive sexual contact.

My ideal of safety and autonomy now is an absolutely monogamous marriage.

For these ex-Other Women, traditional values reassert themselves: monogamy, commitment, trust, and marriage. Having lived in a second world of secrets, lies, and betrayals, with severe pain or disillusionment as the outcome, these women reject the idea of reentering that world or even one similar to it. Although a monogamous marriage, or for that matter any marriage, may be unavailable to them, they would chose "celibacy forever" or impersonal, anonymous sex in preference to another *relationship* based on deceit. They do not simply want to be the first woman in a man's life, they want to be the *only* woman.

These Other Women want "cleaner," more honest relationships with women as well. Through their experiences with married men, they have become more identified with the wife and with women as a group:

I know what it can do to the woman who is married to him, and that, in part, from my own experience when I was left for another woman. And I know the "other woman" always gets hurt. Both women get hurt. Period. I don't think there is any way around that. I can't stand the use of women to empower men against women.

How each woman judges the liaison directly relates to how she has fared within it and what she now wants from her relationships with men and with women. It is somewhat curious, then, that all three categories of women—those who would get involved again, those who would not, and those who are ambivalent—agree on the advice they would offer a women considering such a liaison: "Be careful." The cautionary theme is so persistent it cannot be ignored:

> Be careful. The chances of coming out wonderful and happy are not real high. Women get hurt, particularly, if they are emotionally involved. You've got to be able to live on almost a day-to-day basis and say I'm doing this because it's fun, it's adventurous and it can last a thousand years or it can last a day and I can't predict that and I got to be ready to lose this thing whenever he decides to go. You got to pay the fiddler for the dancing.

> If you like to suffer, if you feel you're a victim and you need someone to hurt you, please be aware of that. It's a perfect set-up. You will hurt.

> I would tell someone about the consequences and you can tell them, like I told myself, never to get involved. I was just going to be friends, meet once in a while, have a few drinks, talk, never meant it to be this way. Part of me thinks that if I could go back and do it over, I would probably let him go. I can't believe that 15 months have gone by, but is it going to be 15 years?

But there is no guarantee that mere caution will prove effective. Single women do not usually act in a risky manner. They do not plan to get involved, nor do they plan to get emotionally attached to their married lovers. But many of them do because the way in which the relationship is socially constructed creates the romantic context in which love feelings surface. Once they are emotionally involved, their secret liaison isolates them from the influence and support of friends, co-workers, and family. She becomes dependent upon her lover, and he can come to control her time schedule, indeed her whole life. Mere individual caution is no barricade.

Because of the demographic, cultural, and social forces at work, single women are going to continue to get involved with married men. Warnings to the contrary are unlikely to be heeded, and advice to be careful is meaningless in practice. Other Women, even those who have thus far gone unscathed, know that pain is a very real possibility in these relationships. The words of caution they proffer are words for themselves as well.

Because women get hurt in and by these relationships does not mean these liaisons will cease. The reverse is true. The ubiquity of relationships between single women and married men is a condition of modern life. It is what Emile Durkheim has referred to as a *social fact*—like marriage, divorce, and suicide.[5] Based on current indicators, somewhere between half and two-thirds of married men are expected to have extramarital liaisons, and most of these will be with single women.[6] There are two major classes of single women primed for these involvements, the "old guard" and the "new recruits." The old guard are women who have come to value their liaisons with married men and see them as a continuing solution to their financial, social, or sexual problems. The new recruits come from two places: Every newly divorced woman is a potential Other Woman. And every single women who has not yet had a relationship with a married man is a potential recruit, especially those older than 25 because their chances for socially approved male companionship lessen with each passing year. As these women grow older, more are likely to consider the married-man solution.

But contemporary women do not become Other Women just because it fulfills their needs: They become other women because it fulfills *husbands'* needs as well. Indeed, the prevalence of the Other Woman phenomenon can be understood in terms of the social functions it *now* performs for males as a *class*.

What do men get from the widespread availability of Other Women? First, of course, is a continuing supply of new sex partners. But there is much more than sex. Relationships with single women give married men an opportunity for intimate female friendship— a person to listen to their grievances and a safe person to be vulnerable to; an opportunity to relive their youth, should they choose a younger woman; and an opportunity to have control over two worlds, their primary one of wives and children and their second, secret one. Sexual gratification, self-esteem, and power—strikingly, these are the very elements of male prerogative which have been challenged over the past 15 years by the women's movement.

Due to feminist imperatives and the economic and social consequences they have engendered, privileges granted to men in the past, simply by virtue of their being male, are eroding. Domestically, as more wives work outside the home and as more of them achieve financial parity with their husbands, a man's rights to determine the rules of the house and the distribution of domestic finances are undermined. Sexually, women have been granted, in principle at least, the right to control their own bodies. Even rape is being legally redefined to accord with women's definitions— imposition against her will—rather than men's. Interpersonally, more women publicly display their preference for female companionship and association and their lack of interest in men's opinions and favors. In his workplace, women are hired as his co-equals and supervisors. Federal laws govern equal opportunity at work and interpret any unasked-for verbal or nonverbal sexual advance as discrimination and sexual harassment. The nation's colleges, graduate schools, and professional schools are burgeoning with female enrollees. In politics and religion, not only do women appear as candidates and ministers, but women's concerns are written into the platforms, sermons, and church by-laws. In brief, wherever a man looks in America today his old world of automatic privilege and power is being undermined by women's entrance and women's successes. Men have been losing the male prerogative. But a married man involved with a single woman can reassert it.

Men, as a group, have had greater economic and social power than women, power which has been sustained by every social institution in America. What men have been losing over the past decade and a half, though, is their *guaranteed* privileged status by virtue of simply *being male.* The phenomenon of the Other Women helps replace some of the ground males have lost.[7]

Since it is in men's interest to have a ready supply of available women—like the industrialists' interest in having a ready supply of expendable labor—it is probable that Other Womanhood will be redefined as simply a fact of life, like being a seasonal or part-time worker. If the stigma lessens, even more women are likely to consider it an option. This is not to say, however, that the role will be condoned. That is unlikely because much of the male's power in the relationship stems from the fact that it is secret and not socially acceptable. The secrecy arising from the stigma of being the "other woman" is what gives the male control over both of his worlds.

Control over both of his worlds is sustained by keeping women separated from each other, by having women view each other as threats, competitors for the same man. Divided, women are conquered. Although a husband may live through great emotional complications and pain, he can have the best of both worlds: his wife and family *and* his secret relationship. His wife at the same time has the lesser of two evils—a tattered marriage or a divorce. If his wife remains ignorant of his relationship, her pain may be minimal, but the issues leading to his infidelity will have been unresolved. He is likely to have more relationships, enhancing his wife's chances for discovery. If she does find out and succeeds in keeping her marriage intact, her victory may be an emotionally hollow one. If divorce is the alternative, she is likely to be left emotionally exhausted and financially disabled.[8] Women are set against women.

For the most part, then, the widespread phenomenon of the Other Woman will contribute to and support the *status quo:* male privilege, the heterosexual imperative, female distrust of other females, and divorce with its attendant social and economic liabilities for women. The "deviant" world of the single woman and the married man is not so deviant after all. Being a part of that world supports, at the personal level, the perpetuation of the social and cultural bulwarks of male privilege.[9]

This does not mean that all single women must or will support the perpetuation of male privilege by being Other Women. Some Other Women, for example, have become "defectors" by rejecting that role for themselves in the future. And some single women are refusing to be recruited. But when married men are excluded from the relationship pool, the supply of men greatly diminishes.

Not only are there not men to marry, there are not even men to "date" illicitly. Under these circumstances, the reality is that the single woman may never marry, or remarry, or ever again have a romantic relationship with a man. With that awareness, some women are beginning to structure their lives as ones to be lived *independently* of a man:

> I am thirty-five years old and there is no man out there for me. It's not just the numbers. It's the quality. I'll have to look to myself.

If a woman believes she will be on her own, the ways in which she organizes her work and intimate relationships will probably change. For example, without a man to fall back on financially, her career may become focal. She may spend more time and energy at work, and receive more success and gratification from it.[10] As men have long known, however, career success and financial solvency cannot substitute for intimate relationships. If there are no available single men of the right type and the married-man solution has been rejected, where might single women find sexual and emotional gratification?

Although women find it difficult, one option is to treat their sexual needs as purely physical, separable from their emotional needs. If they are successful in separating the two in thought and deed, they can look for sexual gratification and emotional gratification in different places. To meet sexual needs, women can turn to improbable partners, persons they see as sexually available but not desirable as long-term lovers. These improbable partners might be men of the "wrong" age, race, or class, or gigolos, or women. A woman executive in her forties has a "twenty-minute stand" with a young soldier; a heterosexual woman "allows" herself to be "picked up in a gay bar by a lesbian"; a thirty-year-old schoolteacher on vacation in Mexico "sleeps with the tour guide." Such encounters might serve to give the woman a sense of greater control over her sexual feelings:

> I can separate sex from love now—something I was not able to do before—and it is the most liberating thing in the world

for me. I can have sex and not feel I'm emotionally bound. I'm more open [to sexual experiences] but less emotionally vulnerable.

But because any sexual encounter with any partner takes time and energy, and carries health, physical, and emotional risks, some single women will choose to meet their sexual needs primarily through sexual fantasy and masturbation. Some aspects of the culture now legitimates female auto-eroticism, as evidenced in the publication of pin-up boy magazines and calendars, how-to-masturbate articles for women, and compilations of women's sexual fantasies, along with the dissemination of Masters and Johnson's research on the speed and intensity of orgasm through self-stimulation. Women can read about or imagine sexual encounters and through masturbation achieve orgasm. One woman half-seriously anthropomorphizes her vibrator:

Tony's always there when I want "him." I just plug him in and he's ready to go when I am. None of this having to please his ego shit before he can get it in.

Not all women will routinely turn to improbable partners or fantasy in order to meet their sexual needs. For some women the separation of sexuality from emotional intimacy may translate into total or near total abstinence from sex, including self-eroticism. Although women today are expected to have sexual urges and sexual desires that they need to have met, many women do not experience those urges or experience them so irregularly and infrequently that they pose no great emergency. Most women have, after all, been reared to repress their sexuality. Celibacy can be viewed as having some positive consequences:

I've been celibate for several years now. Sex is just not very important to me. It's overrated. Without sex, I have more time for myself and what I really value.

I'm finding that being celibate is putting me more in touch with other aspects of my sensuality. I love to swim and love the feeling of the water against my skin.

These sexual options will seem pallid to most women, although they are made more palatable by viewing them as temporary, marking-time activities until an appropriate relationship appears, and not a permanent state. Acting upon the separation of sexual and emotional intimacy while in that "temporary" state may have some positive consequences for women's relationships with women and with their families. If emotional gratification is to be found in nonromantic relationships, spending time and living with female friends might become a purposeful, first choice; women might be highly cherished as the primary and *dependable* sources of warmth, tenderness, and friendship.[11]

Single women might look to other sources for emotional intimacy as well. They could recast themselves into old familial roles such as "the Good Aunt" or "indulgent Grandma," find within their extended families meaningful relationships, and provide close-kin examples of alternative lifestyles for the young. Or the time and energy a single mother might have devoted to finding and keeping a man could be redirected toward her own children, who might, in turn, provide her with warmth and companionship. More radically, a single woman may choose to have a child through adoption or artificial insemination. In our cultural development, sexuality has been increasingly separated from marriage. By separating sexuality from reproduction and reproduction from marriage, these women might be forging new definitions of sexuality and the family.

After all is said and done, though, it is a rare single woman who will find in her work, her friends, her casual sex encounters, her fantasies, and her family—or some combination of these—an adequate substitute for being in a sexual love relationship with a man. Emotional needs are too deep, the cultural dicta too strong, the socialization too repetitive, and the social world too organized around heterosexual couplehood for most women who are not involved with a man to feel "attractive," or "valuable," or "normal."

Because there are not enough single men for the 33 million single women in America today, the options are not great: Many single women are going to be the Other Woman.

Most ironically, yet hopefully, the very women who have rejected the married-man solution and who have accepted the probability that they will live their lives without a romantic attachment to a man are the women most likely to create honest and egalitarian relationships with a man, if and when they should get involved. Because these women are financially and psychologically independent of a man, they do not have to "settle for," to compromise their ideals, to accept "second best." They can enter a relationship as genuine equals. They do not have to be the "new" Other Woman in search of a "good" relationship but caught in a deceitful one, because all by themselves, they already have much of what modern women are looking for: freedom and security.

Appendix

INTERVIEW GUIDE

I am interested, as you know, in your perceptions of your experiences in your relationship. I would like to know how you felt before the relationship began, during the relationship, and, if appropriate, after the relationship, as well as to ask some general questions.

I will use this guide as a kind of check-sheet,—so, I may, near the close of the interview, turn to some questions we have not talked about, as yet.

I'd like you to begin wherever you would like in telling me about your relationship and we'll just go from there. I want to know about *your* experiences and feelings.

A. *Prerelationship*

How would you describe what you were feeling, doing, etc., prior to the beginning of the relationship? (Role transitions?)
  a. Age
  b. Marital status
  c. Previous marital history
  d. Parental obligations, if any
  e. Occupational status
  f. Educational status
  g. Place of residence

B.   *Getting Into the Relationship*

How did you meet?

What were your first impressions? What kind of person was he? How would you describe him?

How long after you knew each other did you first believe that there was potentially a stronger liaison between you?

How did you know? What were the cues?

How did you handle those first thoughts or ideas? (Reject them, embrace them, seek advice, etc.?)

How did the possibility of the relationship get raised? (Through one of you, verbally, nonverbally, etc.?)

What were your feelings at this point?

What were your expectations? (Short-term, long-lasting, etc.?)

About how much time passed between the first thoughts and the relationship beginning? Did you consider a sexual liaison in the beginning?

Did you know his marital status?

C.   *Maintaining the Relationship*

How much time do/did you spend together?

How do/did you spend most of your time together? What do/did you do?

Has/Did his/your level of commitment changed/change?

Have/Did your own expectations altered/alter?

Have/Did his?

Do/Did you talk much about his marriage? Wife? Children?

What things do/did you like best about the relationship?

What things do/did you find most troublesome?

    Probe: negotiating differing levels of commitment
           negotiating different sets of expectations
           holidays, special events
           gift-giving
           contacting each other
           children: yours/his

Who knows/knew about your relationship? Friends? (His? Yours?) Family members? (His? Yours?) Co-workers? (His? Yours?) His wife?

When and how did they find out?

What were their responses? (Supportive?)

How do/did you handle other people's knowledge about your relationship?

What are/were your feelings about his wife? How do/did you handle
those?

Are/were you monogamous?

How would you evaluate the sexual aspect of your relationship?

If a feminist, how does/did your feminist ideology affect your relationship?

D. *Terminating the Relationship* (if appropriate)

How long did the relationship continue?

How did it terminate?

Did he leave his wife?

Who initiated terminating the relationship?

How? Were there cues you picked up that suggested it was ending?

If you were to write an epitaph for this relationship, what would it say?

Would you do it again?

Is there anything else about this relationship that you think I should
know about?

E. *Aftermath* (if appropriate)

How would you characterize your current relationships with men? With
women?

Attitudes toward marriage? Work? Males? Females?

F. *General*

Why do you think most women enter these relationships?

What do you think they get from them?

Do you think there are any particular kinds of women who are more
likely to get involved? If so, what kinds of women?

Why do you think men enter these relationships?

Are there any particular kinds of men that you think are more likely
to? Can you describe them?

What advice would you give a woman contemplating such a relationship?

Would you have another relationship with a married man?

How would you characterize this relationship in contrast to your relationships with single men?

Why do you think some extramarital relationships are casual one-night
type liaisons, and others are more involved and committed?

Do you think the one-night stand is "safe"?

G. *Current Demographic Information*

    a. Age
    b. Marital status
    c. Occupation
    d. Education
    e. Parental status
    f. Residence

H. *Anything Else?*

May I call you again if I need to? Please don't hesitate contacting me. Thank you *very* much.

Notes

Chapter One. The Other Woman Phenomenon

1. There are "how-to" mass market books, books of literary criticism, and fiction on the Other Woman but *no* social-scientific research from the perspective of the single woman other than the papers written by this author. Reviews of the sociological research literature on extra-marital relationships can be found in: Anthony B. Thompson, "Extramarital Sex: A Review of the Research Literature," *The Journal of Sex Research* 19(1), 1983, pp. 1–22; Lynn Atwater, *The Extramarital Connection: Sex, Intimacy, and Identity* (New York: Irvington, 1982), pp. 15–29; Roger W. Libby, "Extramarital and Comarital Sex: A Critique of the Literature," in Roger W. Libby and Robert N. Whitehurst (eds.), *Marriage and Its Alternatives: Exploring Intimate Life Styles* (Glencoe, Ill.: Scott, Foresman, 1977), pp. 80–111.

2. Thompson, op. cit.

3. Anthony Pietropinto and Jacqueline Simenaur, *Beyond the Male Myth* (New York: New American Library, 1977), p. 311.

4. Ira L. Reiss, R. E. Anderson, and G. C. Sponaugle, "A Multivariate Model of the Determinants of Extramarital Sexual Permissiveness," *Journal of Marriage and the Family* 42, 1980, pp. 395–411; Thompson, op. cit., p. 17.

5. Gilbert D. Nass, Roger W. Libby, and Mary Pat Fisher, *Sexual Choices* (Belmont, Cal.: Wadsworth, 1981), p. 270.

6. There is scant knowledge on what proportion of men's extramarital

relationships are with single women. The lack of knowledge is an indicator of how the single woman's experiences have been disregarded by normative sociological research. Although surveys on sexual behavior are routinely administered to the general population, to the best of my knowledge no one has asked married men whether their extramarital partners are single or married. Lewis Yablonsky, in *The Extra-Sex Factor* (New York: Times Books, 1979), estimated that 54% of the women were single; Melissa Sands, founder of *Mistresses Anonymous*, estimates that 75% of "mistresses" are single women. See Melissa Sands, "When Women Have Affairs . . . Myths about 'Mistresses,' " *MS. Magazine*, November 1981, p. 116. Since the number of single women has grown dramatically since Yablonsky's research, his numbers are probably underestimates. Moreover, because wives have husbands, sociologically they are not so much Other Women as they are wives engaged in extramarital sex. It is a very different experience to be a wife who has a lover than it is to be a single woman whose lover has a wife. In this book, I choose to focus only on the latter experience.

7. Marcia Guttentag and Paul Secord, *Too Many Women? The Sex Ratio Question* (Beverly Hills, Ca.: Sage, 1983), pp. 14–16. Also see Joan Huber and Glenna Spitze, *Sex Stratification: Children, Housework, Jobs* (New York: Academic Press, 1983).

8. Peter Stein, "Understanding Single Adulthood," in Peter Stein (ed.), *Single Life: Unmarried Adults in Social Context* (New York: St. Martin's, 1981), p. 9.

9. Noreen Goldman, Charles Westoff, and Charles Hammerslough, "Demography of the Marriage Market in the United States," *Population Index* 50 (1), 1984, pp. 5–25.

10. Ibid., p. 16.

11. Arlene Saluter, "Marital Status and Living Arrangements: March, 1983," *Current Population Reports, Population Characteristics*, Series P-20, No. 389, issued June, 1983. Washington, D. C.: Bureau of the Census.

12. Goldman, Westoff, and Hammerslough, op. cit., p. 16.

13. Phillip Blumstein and Pepper Schwartz, *American Couples: Money, Work, Sex* (New York: William Morrow, 1983), p. 32.

14. Goldman, Westoff and, Hammerslough, op. cit., p. 15.

15. Blumstein and Schwartz, op. cit., p. 32.

16. Andrew Hacker (ed.), *U/S: A Statistical Portrait of the American People* (New York: Viking, 1983), p. 112.

17. These sex differences in the estimates of the incidence of homosexuality have remained fairly constant since Kinsey's original research in the late 1940s, although surveys on the topic have been rare. Ian

Robertson, in *Sociology* (New York: Worth, 1977), reports that although 28% of women have lesbian experiences, only 4% identify themselves as lesbians.

18. Christine Doudna (with Fern McBride), "Where Are the Men for the Women at the Top?", in Peter Stein (ed.), op. cit., p. 23. Black women have experienced this problem for decades due to the differential educational attainment level of black women and black men.

19. Blumstein and Schwartz, op. cit., p. 32.

20. In 1982 there were 15,262 million never-married women over age 18; 10,795 million widows; and 6,895 million divorcées. U. S. Bureau of the Census, *Statistical Abstracts of the United States, 1984* (Washington, D. C.: U. S. Government Printing Office, 1984), Table 51, p. 49.

21. Goldman, Westoff, and Hammerslough, op. cit., p. 20.

22. Doudna, op. cit., p. 22.

23. Guttentag and Secord, op. cit., pp. 161–7. For a more general discussion of power and dependency in male-female relationships, see Peter Blau, *Exchange and Power in Social Life* (New York: Wiley, 1964).

24. Barbara Ehrenreich, *The Hearts of Men: American Dreams and the Flight from Commitment* (Garden City, N. Y.: Doubleday, 1983).

25. For an excellent discussion of the meaning and power of the heterosexual ideology, see Adrienne Rich, "Compulsory Heterosexuality and Lesbian Existence," *Signs* 5 (Summer), 1980, pp. 631–660. For a more general sociological discussion, see Laurel Richardson, *The Dynamics of Sex and Gender: A Sociological Perspective* (Boston: Houghton, 1981), pp. 9–17.

26. Robert K. Merton in two companion papers, "Social Structure and Anomie" and "Continuities in the Theory of Social Structure and Anomie," in Robert K. Merton, *Social Theory and Social Structure* (New York: Free Press, 1957), pp. 131–194, argued that if goals were inculcated but the means to those goals thwarted, people would use illegitimate means to achieve the socially approved ends. Deviance, he argued, was socially induced. In the application of his theory, he looked at how financial success norms led to delinquency. In his analysis, women were invisible; he was writing about expectations for men only and the origins of male deviance. What I am proposing here is that Merton's typology of adaptation (see Merton, p. 140) might be applied to women: being an Other Woman is structurally induced. Atwater, op. cit., 1982, has a similar implicit analysis about wives who have extramarital relationships. She refers to them as "innovators," one of Merton's types.

27. For readers who are either interested in the lesbian alternative or doubt its facticity, there are currently over fifty periodicals and news-

letters written expressly for and by lesbians or women-identified-women, more than 1000 clubs and organizations for lesbians, over 100 lesbian-feminist bookstores, as well as hundreds of women-only coffeehouses, vacation resorts, and retreats. A new periodical, *The Journal of Celibacy*, which is primarily personal accounts of the celibate choice, is now available, and *Off Our Backs*, one of the oldest feminist periodicals in the United States, from time to time discusses the celibate alternative.

28. For an analysis of the impact of the women's movement on women's lives, see Verta Taylor, "The Future of Feminism in the 1980s: A Social Movement Analysis," in Laurel Richardson and Verta Taylor (eds.), *Feminist Frontiers: Rethinking Sex, Gender, and Society* (Boston, Mass.: Addison-Wesley, 1983), pp. 434–451.

29. The Harris Poll reported in *The Washington Post*, June 11, 1984.

30. Jacqueline Simenauer and David Carroll, *Singles: The New Americans* (New York: New American Library, 1982).

31. Karl King, Jack O. Balswick, and Ira E. Robinson, "The Continuing Premarital Sexual Revolution Among College Females." *Journal of Marriage and the Family*, August 1977, pp. 455–459. This convergence toward a single premarital sexual standard was first predicted by Ira L. Reiss in *Premarital Sexual Standards in America* (New York: Free Press, 1960).

32. Karl King et al., ibid., p. 456.

33. Personal communication, Ira L. Reiss, specialist in research on extra-marital sex attitudes and behavior, February 1985.

34. Ira L. Reiss, *Family Systems in America*, 3rd edn., (New York: Holt, 1980), p. 175.

35. Beth B. Hess, Elizabeth W. Markson, and Peter Stein, *Sociology* (New York: Macmillan, 1985).

36. Ira L. Reiss and Brent C. Miller, "Heterosexual Permissiveness: A Theoretical Analysis," in W. Burr, R. Hill, I. Nye, and I. Reiss (eds.), *Contemporary Theories about the Family*, Vol. 1 (New York: Free Press, 1979), pp. 57–100.

37. See Lillian B. Rubin, *Intimate Strangers: Men and Women Together* (New York: Harper, 1983); Ann Swidler, "Love and Adulthood in American Culture," in Neil Smelser and Erik Eriksen (eds.), *Theories of Work and Love in America* (Cambridge, Mass.: Harvard U. P., 1980), pp. 120–147.

38. Rachel M. Brownstein, *Becoming a Heroine: Reading about Women in Novels* (New York: Penguin, 1984).

39. Brownstein, ibid., p. xvii.

40. For a discussion of emotions as "women's work," see Arlie Russell Hochschild, *The Managed Heart: Commercialization of Human Feeling* (Berkeley: U. of California P., 1983).

41. For a general sociological discussion of role strain and role prolifera-
tion, see Sheldon Stryker and Anne Statham, "Symbolic Interaction
and Role Theory," in Gardner Lindzey (ed.), *Handbook of Social Psychology*
1985 (forthcoming). For autobiographical accounts of women's role
strains, see Sara Ruddick and Pamela Daniel (eds.), *Working It Out*
(New York: Pantheon, 1977). For a theoretical analysis of role transitions, see Lucinda SanGiovanni, *Ex-Nuns: A Study of Emergent Role Passage*
(Norwood, N. J.: Ablex, 1978). For a sociological-autobiographical
account of this process, see Joan Huber, "Ambiguities in Identity
Transformation: from Sugar and Spice to Professor," in Richardson
and Taylor (eds.), op. cit., pp. 330–337.

42. Hacker (ed.), op. cit., chapter 11.

43. Anne Statham, "Women and Men Supervisors and Their Secretaries:
The Implications of Sex Differences in Managerial Styles," unpublished manuscript, University of Wisconsin-Parkside, 1984.

44. For a discussion of labeling theory and its application to women,
see Edwin M. Schur, *Labeling Women Deviant: Gender, Stigma, and Social
Control* (New York: Random, 1984).

45. For a review of the theoretical and research literature on the structure
of gender inequality, see Richardson, op. cit., pp. 171–246; also see
Jean Lipman-Blumen, *Gender Roles and Power* (Englewood Cliffs, N. J.:
Prentice-Hall, 1984).

46. For a review of some of the psychological theories of extramarital
relationships and their applications, see Herbert S. Strean, *The Extramarital Affair* (New York: Free Press, 1980).

47. The idea that larger social truths are often embedded in what appears
to be nonnormative has a long intellectual history within sociology.
For example, see Georg Simmel in Kurt H. Wolff (trans. and ed.),
The Sociology of Georg Simmel (New York: Free Press, 1950); for an ethno-
methodological argument and application, see Harold Garfinkel, *Studies
in Ethnomethodology* (Englewood Cliffs, N. J.: Prentice-Hall, 1968); for
a radical feminist perspective, see Kathleen Barry, "Female Sexual
Slavery," in Alison M. Jagger and Paula S. Rothenberg (eds.) *Feminist
Frameworks* (New York: McGraw-Hill, 1984), pp. 405–416.

Chapter Two. Getting Involved

1. When I began this study, I interviewed ten of the married men involved with the single women I had interviewed; eight of these men
denied any premeditated intentions of getting involved. For a review
of the literature on husbands' extramarital relationships, see Anthony
B. Thompson, "Extramarital Sex: A Review of the Research Litera-

ture," *The Journal of Sex Research* 19(1), 1983, pp. 1–22. In contrast to the single women in this study, Lynn Atwater in *The Extramarital Connection: Sex, Intimacy, and Identity* (New York: Irvington, 1982), reports that married women who have extramarital relationships are more likely to be "looking" for them.

2. For a discussion of this issue see David L. Bradford, Alice G. Sargent, and Melinda S. Sprague, "The Executive Man and Woman: the Issue of Sexuality," in Dail Ann Neugarten and Jay M. Shafritz (eds.), *Sexuality in Organizations: Romantic and Coercive Behaviors at Work* (Oak Park, Ill.: Moore, 1980), pp. 17–28. Also see Erving Goffman, *Gender Advertisements* (New York: Harper, 1976); Arlene Kaplan Daniels, "The Low-Caste Stranger in Social Research," in Gideon Sjoberg (ed.), *Ethics, Politics, and Social Research* (Cambridge, Mass.: Scherkman, 1967), pp. 267–296.

3. Adrienne Rich, "Compulsory Heterosexuality and Lesbian Existence," *Signs* 5 (Summer), 1980, pp. 631–660.

4. See Constantina Safilios-Rothschild, *Love, Sex, and Sex Roles* (Englewood Cliffs, N. J.: Prentice-Hall, 1977); Hans L. Zetterberg, "The Secret Ranking," *Journal of Marriage and the Family* 28(2), 1966, pp. 161–166.

5. Elaine G. Walster, William Walster, Jane Piliavin, and Lynn Schmidt, "Playing Hard to Get: Understanding an Elusive Phenomenon," *Journal of Personality and Social Psychology* 26(2), 1973, pp. 113–121.

6. For a discussion of male-female sexuality and sociability see Safilios-Rothschild, *Love, Sex, and Sex Roles.* A superb analysis of heterosexuality norms based on participant observation is available in Judith A. Di-Iorio, "Nomad Vans and Lady Vanners: A Critical Feminist Analysis of a Van Club," PhD dissertation, The Ohio State University, Columbus, Ohio, 1982; also see the groundbreaking work of Sherri Cavan, *Liquor License: An Ethnography of Bar Behavior* (Chicago: Aldine, 1966).

7. In an exploratory study, I asked 400 introductory sociology students to complete a story. Half of the students were given as the first line of the story, "Jane, who is single, is having a relationship with Joe, who is married." The other half were given the line, "Jane, who is married, is having a relationship with Joe, who is single." Nearly all the male students wrote a violent ending to the married woman/single man story, but not to the single woman/married man one. In addition, some state laws have given husbands the legal right to kill any man who fornicates with his wife, and rape laws have been based on the husband's exclusive rights to his sexual property, his wife. I suspect the threat of violence between men as a social control mechanism is probably stronger even than I have described it in the text.

8. Catherine A. MacKinnon, *Sexual Harassment of Working Women: A Case*

of Sex Discrimination (New Haven, Conn.: Yale U. P., 1979); Neugarten and Shafritz (eds.), op. cit.

9. Michael Korda, *Male Chauvinism: How It Works* (New York: Random, 1973), pp. 17–68.

10. Robert K. Merton, "The Self-Fulfilling Prophecy," in Robert K. Merton, *Social Theory and Social Structure* (New York: Free Press, 1957), pp. 421–436.

11. Bradford, Sargent, and Sprague, op. cit.

12. For a sociological anthology on single life, see Peter Stein, (ed.), *Single Life: Unmarried Adults in Social Context* (New York: St. Martin's, 1981); for a review of the sociological research, see Leonard Cargan, *Singles: Myths and Realities* (Beverly Hills, Ca.: Sage, 1982).

13. For an analysis of unexpected encounters, see Safilios-Rothschild, op. cit., chapter 5.

14. Jessie Bernard introduced the idea of "his" and "her" reality into the literature by noting that "his" and "her" marriages are different in "The Paradox of the Happy Marriage," in Vivian Gornick and Barbara Moran (eds.), *Women in Sexist Society: Studies in Power and Powerlessness* (New York: New American Library, 1971), pp. 145–163.

15. The most ingenious and convincing study of these differences in meanings can be found in John Timothy Diamond, "On the Social Structure of Imagery: The Case of Gender" PhD dissertation, The Ohio State University, Columbus, Ohio, 1977. Diamond used the game of charades to display how the same words conjured up different images in men and women.

16. The most complete review of the research on friendship and gender, as well as an extensive bibliography on the subject, can be found in Robert R. Bell, *Worlds of Friendship* (Beverly Hills, Ca.: Sage, 1981). Also see Paul H. Wright, "Men's Friendships, Women's Friendships, and the Alleged Inferiority of the Latter," *Sex Roles* 8, 1982, pp. 1–21; Beth B. Hess, "Friendship and Gender Roles Over the Life Course," in Stein (ed.), op. cit., pp. 104–115; Janet Lever, "Sex Differences in the Games Children Play," *Social Problems* 23, 1976, pp. 478–487; Janet Lever, "Sex Differences in the Complexity of Children's Play and Games," *American Sociological Review* 43, 1978, pp. 471–483; Janet Less Barkas, *Friendship Throughout Life* (New York: Public Affairs Pamphlets, 1983); Scott O. Swain, "Male Intimacy in Same-Sex Friendship: The Impact of Gender-Validating Activities," presented to the American Sociological Association Meetings, San Francisco, August 1984.

17. For an analysis of the relationship between sexuality, sexual harassment, and the economic subordination of women, see MacKinnon, op. cit.; also see Neugarten and Shafritz (eds.), op. cit.

18. Carol Gilligan, *In a Different Voice: Psychological Theory and Women's Development* (Cambridge, Mass.: Harvard U. P., 1982).

19. The classic analysis of this general phenomenon, the propensity of people to normalize situations, was done by Joan Emerson; for experimental research demonstrating that propensity, see Bibb Latané and John M. Darley, "Bystander Apathy," *American Scientist* 57, 1969, pp. 224–268.

Chapter Three. Having Sex

1. For example, see a review of literature in Roger W. Libby, "Extramarital and Comarital Sex: A Critique of the Literature," in Roger W. Libby and Robert N. Whitehurst (eds.), *Marriage and Its Alternatives: Exploring Intimate Life Styles* (Glencoe, Ill.: Scott, Foresman, 1977), pp. 80–111; Anthony B. Thompson, "Extramarital Sex: A Review of the Research Literature," *The Journal of Sex Research* 19 (1), 1983, pp. 1–22. But, also see Lynn Atwater, *The Extramarital Connection: Sex, Intimacy, and Identity* (New York: Irvington, 1982).

2. Maurice North and Frederick Taoles, "Is Adultery Biological?" *New Society* 21 (772), 1977, pp. 125–126.

3. For an excellent analysis of the antifeminist backlash movements, see Barbara Ehrenreich, *The Hearts of Men: American Dreams and the Flight from Commitment* (Garden City, N. Y.: Doubleday, 1983).

4. Lois S. Bird, *How to Be a Happily Married Mistress* (Garden City, N. Y.: Doubleday, 1970). For an analysis of advice books, see Michael Gordon and Penelope Shankweiler, "Different Equals Less: Female Sexuality in Recent Marriage Manuals," *Journal of Marriage and the Family* 33, 1971, pp. 459–466; also see Meryl Altman, "Everything They Always Wanted You to Know: The Ideology of Popular Sex," in Carole S. Vance (ed.), *Pleasure and Danger: Exploring Female Sexuality* (Boston: Routledge and Kegan Paul, 1984).

5. Constantina Safilios-Rothschild, *Love, Sex, and Sex Roles* (Englewood Cliffs, N. J.: Prentice-Hall, 1977). For analyses of sex and other power issues see Ann Snitow, Christine Stansall, and Sharon Thompson (eds.), *Powers of Desire: The Politics of Sexuality* (New York: Monthly Review Press, 1983); and Vance (ed.), op. cit.

6. For analyses of how sex-stereotypes become reified, see Judith A. DiIorio, "Nomad Vans and Lady Vanners: A Critical Feminist Analysis of a Van Club," PhD dissertation, The Ohio State University, Columbus, Ohio, 1982; Margrit Eichler, *The Double Standard: A Feminist Critique of Feminist Social Science* (New York: St. Martin's, 1980).

7. For a psychoanalytic-sociological discussion of how mothers repro-

duce themselves in their daughters, see Nancy Chodorow, *The Reproduction of Mothering: Psychoanalysis and the Sociology of Gender* (Berkeley, Ca.: U. of California P., 1978). Also see Mary S. Calderone, "Above and Beyond Politics: The Sexual Socialization of Children," in Vance (ed.), op. cit.

8. For an analysis of sexual exchanges from a labeling perspective, see Jacqueline P. Wiseman, "Sex as a Personal and Social Phenomenon," in Wiseman (ed.), *The Social Psychology of Sex* (New York: Harper, 1976), pp. 1–16. For an excellent discussion of the effects of labeling sexual activities as deviant, see Edwin M. Schur, *Labeling Women Deviant: Gender, Stigma, and Social Control* (New York: Random, 1984). For a more specific discussion of vacillation in the negotiation of sexual exchanges, see Wiseman, op. cit., p. 12.

9. Many lesbians in the 1950s were so concerned with appearing "normal" that they adopted the sex-stereotyped roles of "butch" (male) and "femme" (female). According to accounts of lesbians during that era, although they knew they were violating sexual norms, they were determined not to violate the "regular" male-female patterns of interaction within their own relationships.

10. Elizabeth Grauerholz, "Initiation and Response: The Dynamics of Sexual Interaction," unpublished paper, Indiana University, Bloomington, Ind., September 1983.

11. Ibid., p. 16.

12. Nancy M. Henley, *Body Politics: Power, Sex, and Nonverbal Communication* (Englewood Cliffs, N. J.: Prentice-Hall, 1977). Also see Erving Goffman, *Gender Advertisements* (New York: Harper, 1976).

13. Beth B. Hess, "Friendship and Gender Roles over the Life Course," in Peter Stein (ed.), *Single Life: Unmarried Adults in Social Context* (New York: St. Martin's, 1981), pp. 104–115; Janet Less Barkas, *Friendship throughout Life* (New York: Public Affairs Pamphlets, 1983); Paul H. Wright, "Men's Friendships, Women's Friendships, and the Alleged Inferiority of the Latter," *Sex Roles* 8 (1982), pp. 1–21; Scott O. Swain, "Male Intimacy in Same-Sex Friendship: The Impact of Gender-Validating Activities," presented to the American Sociological Association Meetings, San Francisco, August 1984.

14. This norm is, of course, represented in the legal precedents that hold that a husband cannot rape his wife; that a prostitute cannot be raped; that a woman who has once slept with a man cannot be raped by him. Only very recently have these ideas been successfully challenged in the courts, and in some states the laws have been changed.

15. See Jacqueline P. Wiseman, "Sex as a Personal and Social Phenomenon," in Wiseman (ed.), op. cit., pp. 10–16. For a more general discus-

sion of how gender restricts sexual roles, see Sheldon Stryker, *Symbolic Interactionism: A Social Structural Version* (Menlo Park, Ca.: Benjamin/Cummings, 1980).

16. Judith Long Laws and Pepper Schwartz, *Sexual Scripts: The Social Construction of Female Sexuality* (Hinsdale, Ill.: Dryden, 1977), p. 62.

Chapter Four. Could This Be Love?

1. See Peter L. Berger, *Invitation to Sociology: A Humanistic Perspective* (New York: Doubleday, 1963), pp. 35–36. For a more recent and longer analysis see Carol Cassell, *Swept Away: Why Women Fear Their Own Sexuality* (New York: Simon & Schuster, 1984).

2. Keith Thomas, *Religion and the Decline of Magic* (New York: Penguin, 1980), pp. 277–278, 373–374.

3. Jacqueline Sarsby, *Romantic Love and Society: Its Place in the Modern World* (New York: Penguin, 1983); Jessie Bernard, "The Paradox of the Happy Marriage," in Vivian Gornik and Barbara Moran (eds.), *Women in Sexist Society: Studies in Power and Powerlessness* (New York: New American Library, 1971), pp. 145–163.

4. See Sidney M. Jourard, *The Transparent Self* (New York: Van Nostrand, 1964); Paul C. Cozby, "Self-Disclosure: A Literature Review," *Psychological Bulletin,* 79, 1973, pp. 73–91; Marilyn Lester, "Making Music Together: A Sociological Formulation of Intimate Encounters Between Males and Females," presented to the American Sociological Association Meetings, Boston, Mass., August 1979; Lillian B. Rubin, *Intimate Strangers: Men and Women Together* (New York: Harper, 1983).

5. Georg Simmel, in Kurt H. Wolff (trans. and ed.), *The Sociology of Georg Simmel* (New York: Free Press, 1950), p. 330.

6. See Mary Cunningham, *Power Play: What Really Happened at Bendix* (New York: Simon & Schuster, 1984).

7. Simmel, op. cit.

8. Lillian Rubin, op. cit., pp. 1–15.

9. Constantina Safilios-Rothschild, *Love, Sex, and Sex Roles* (Englewood Cliffs, N. J.: Prentice-Hall, 1977), pp. 77–79.

10. Simmel, op. cit., p. 348.

11. See, for example, Anne Statham (Macke) and Laurel Richardson (with Judith A. Cook), *Sex-Typed Teaching Styles of University Professors and Student Reactions* (Washington, D. C.: National Institute of Education, 1980); Joan M. Patterson and Hamilton I. McCubbin, "Gender Roles and Coping," *Journal of Marriage and the Family* 46, February 1984, pp. 95–104; Jeanne Parr Lemkau, "Personality and Background Characteristics

of Women in Male-Dominated Occupations: A Review," *Psychology of Women Quarterly* 4 (2), 1979, pp. 221–240; Eleanor Berman, "What Working Women Tell their Therapists," *Working Mother,* March 1984, pp. 29–32. Also see Peggy McIntosh, "Feeling Like a Fraud," unpublished paper, Center for Research on Women, Wellesley College, 1984.

12. See, for example, Anne Statham, "Women and Men Supervisors and Their Secretaries: The Implications of Sex Differences in Managerial Styles," unpublished manuscript, University of Wisconsin-Parkside, 1984.

13. Jourard, 1964; Sidney Jourard, *Self-Disclosure: An Experimental Analysis of the Transparent Self* (New York: Wiley-Interscience, 1971); Judith Milstein Zatz, "How Do You Love Me? Let Me Count the Ways (the Phenomenology of Being Loved)," *Sociological Inquiry* 46, 1976, pp. 17–22; Lillian Rubin, op. cit.; Lester, op. cit.

14. Paul C. Cozby, "Self-Disclosure: a Literature Review," *Psychological Bulletin* 79, 1973, pp. 73–91; Lester, op. cit.; Zick Rubin, "Lovers and Other Strangers: The Development of Intimacy in Encounters and Relationships," *American Scientist* 62, 1974, pp. 182–190.

15. Peter L. Berger and Hans F. Kellner, "Marriage and the Construction of Reality," *Diogenes* 46, 1964, pp. 1–25.

16. Zick Rubin, op. cit.

Chapter Five.   Concealing and Revealing

1. An excellent discussion of reconstructive biography—how people rewrite their biographies based on their current position in life—is available in Peter L. Berger, *Invitation to Sociology: A Humanistic Perspective* (Garden City, N. Y.: Doubleday, 1963), pp. 54–65.

2. Anne Statham (Macke) and Laurel Richardson (with Judith A. Cook), *Sex-Typed Teaching Styles of University Professors and Student Reactions* (Washington, D. C.: National Institute of Education, 1980); Cynthia Epstein, *Women's Place: Options and Limits on a Professional Career* (Berkeley, Ca.: U. of California P., 1970).

3. Georg Simmel, in Kurt H. Wolff (trans. and ed.), *The Sociology of Georg Simmel* (New York: Free Press, 1950), pp. 307–355.

4. For a general sociological discussion of the stranger, see Simmel, op. cit., pp. 402–409.

5. See David McClelland, *Power: The Inner Experience* (New York: Irvington, 1975). People who have high power needs—needs to control others—

are more likely to take risks than people who do not have these needs. Men are more strongly motivated to achieve power than women.

6. For an analysis of lesbian coming-out, see Ruth Baetz, "The Coming-Out Process: Violence Against Lesbians," in Trudy Darty and Sandee Potter (eds.), *Women-Identified-Women* (Palo Alto, Ca.: Mayfield, 1984), pp. 51–67.

7. The idea of the "spoiled status" is from Erving Goffman, *Stigma: Notes on the Management of Spoiled Identity* (Englewood Cliffs, N. J.: Prentice-Hall, 1963).

8. Dair L. Gillespie, "Who Has the Power? The Marital Struggle," *Journal of Marriage and the Family* 33, 1971, pp. 445–58.

9. Ibid.

Chapter Six.   His Wife

1. For reviews of the coping literature see: Elizabeth G. Menaghan, "Individual Coping Efforts: Moderators of the Relationship Between Life Stress and Mental Health Outcomes," in Howard B. Kaplan (ed.), *Psychological Stress: Trends in Theory and Research* (New York: Academic, 1983), pp. 157–189; Rudolph H. Moos and Andrew G. Billings, "Conceptualizing and Measuring Coping Resources and Processes," in Leo Goldberger and Shlomo Breznitz (eds.), *Handbook of Stress: Theoretical and Clinical Aspects* (New York: Free Press, 1982), pp. 212–230.

2. Lynn Atwater, *The Extramarital Connection: Sex, Intimacy, and Identity* (New York: Irvington, 1982), reports that the married women she studied who were having extramarital relationships did not express guilt, either. Also see Graham B. Spanier and Randie L. Margolis, "Marital Separation and Extramarital Sexual Behavior," *The Journal of Sex Research* 19, 1983, pp. 23–48. Spanier and Margolis conclude that there is no correlation between the presence or absence of an extramarital relationship and marital quality at time of separation. Also see Phillip Blumstein and Pepper Schwartz, *American Couples: Money, Work, Sex* (New York: Morrow, 1983).

3. Barbara Ehrenreich, *The Hearts of Men: American Dreams and the Flight from Commitment* (Garden City, N. Y.: Doubleday, 1983), pp. 88–99.

4. For example see Phillip L. Elbaum, "The Dynamics, Implications, and Treatment of Extramarital Sexual Relationships for the Family Therapist," *Journal of Marital and Family Therapy* 7, 1981, pp. 489–495.

5. Since women were interviewed at various stages in their relationships and some of them at regular intervals during their relationships, and

since their interpretations were so similar, it is unlikely that the women can be accused of falsely reconstructing their biographies.

6. Denial of culpability, denial of the wife's existence, and compartmentalizing strategies are examples of "suppression" coping efforts. In general, these coping efforts can be relatively successful in managing emotions. See Menaghan, op. cit.

7. Shirley Eskapa, *Woman Versus Woman: The Extramarital Affair* (New York: Franklin Watts, 1984).

8. Discounting, competing, blaming, and helping can be thought of as "optimistic comparison" coping efforts. In general, optimistic comparisons are fairly effective. See Menaghan, op. cit.

9. Eskapa, op. cit., p. 57.

10. For a discussion of the ideology of the women's movement, see Verta Taylor, "The Future of Feminism in the 1980s: A Social Movement Analysis," in Laurel Richardson and Verta Taylor (eds.), *Feminist Frontiers: Rethinking Sex, Gender, and Society* (Boston, Mass.: Addison-Wesley, 1983), pp. 434–451.

Chapter Seven. Feeling Bad

1. Laurel (Walum) Richardson, *The Dynamics of Sex and Gender: A Sociological Perspective* (Boston: Houghton, 1981), pp. 17–36.

2. Nancy M. Henley, *Body Politics: Power, Sex, and Nonverbal Communication* (Englewood Cliffs, N. J.: Prentice-Hall, 1977).

3. Candace West, "Against Our Will; Male Interruptions of Female Conversations in Cross-Sex Conversation," in Judith Orasnu, Mariam K. Slater, and Lenore Loeb Adler (eds.), *Language, Sex and Gender: Does La Différence Make a Difference?* (New York: New York Academy of Sciences Annals, 1979), pp. 81–100.

4. See John A. Phillips, *Eve: The History of an Idea* (New York: Harper, 1984).

5. Unfaithful spouses are more likely to imagine their partners are also unfaithful. See Virginia Adams, "Getting at the Heart of Jealous Love," in Robert H. Walsh and Ollie Pocs (eds.), *Marriage and Family 82/83* (Guilford, Conn.: Annual Editions, Dushkin, 1982), p. 40.

6. For example, see Debra Kalmuss and Murray Straus, "Wives' Marital Dependency and Wife Abuse," *Journal of Marriage and the Family* 44, 1982, pp. 277–286; Murray Straus, Richard Gelles, and S. Steinmetz, *Behind Closed Doors: Violence in the American Family* (Garden City, N. Y.: Doubleday, 1980).

7. Adams, op. cit., p. 40.

8. Ibid., p. 41.

9. Ibid., p. 42.

10. Elizabeth G. Menaghan, "Individual Coping Efforts: Moderators of the Relationship Between Life Stress and Mental Health Outcomes," in Howard B. Kaplan (ed.), *Psychological Stress: Trends in Theory and Research* (New York: Academic, 1983).

Chapter Eight. Endings

1. Georg Simmel, in Kurt H. Wolff (trans. and ed.), *The Sociology of Georg Simmel* (New York: Free Press, 1950), p. 124.

2. Graham B. Spanier and Randie L. Margolis, "Marital Separation and Extramarital Sexual Behavior," *The Journal of Sex Research* 19, 1983, pp. 23–48, discuss the role of extramarital sex in marital separation.

3. Shirley Eskapa, *Woman Versus Woman: The Extramarital Affair* (New York: Franklin Watts, 1984); George Levinger, "A Social Psychological Perspective on Marital Dissolution," in George Levinger and Oliver C. Moles (eds.), *Divorce and Separation: Context, Causes, and Consequences* (New York: Basic, 1979), pp. 37–60.

4. Eskapa, ibid.; Jessie Bernard, "Foreword" in Levinger and Moles (eds.), op. cit., pp. ix–xv.

5. Levinger, op. cit.

6. Daniel J. Levinson, *The Seasons of a Man's Life* (New York: Knopf, 1978); also see Gail Sheehy, *Passages: Predictable Crises of Adult Life* (New York: Dutton, 1976).

7. Virginia Adams, "Getting at the Heart of Jealous Love," in Robert H. Walsh and Ollie Pocs (eds.), *Marriage and Family 82/83* (Guilford, Conn.: Annual Editions, Dushkin, 1982), pp. 39–44.

8. Peter Blau, *Exchange and Power in Social Life* (New York: Wiley, 1964).

9. Charles T. Hill, Zick Rubin, and Letitia Anne Peplau, "Breakups Before Marriage: The End of 103 Affairs," in Levinger and Moles (eds.), op. cit., pp. 64–82.

10. Arlie Russell Hochschild, *The Managed Heart: Commercialization of Human Feeling* (Berkeley: U. of California P., 1983).

11. For a review of the bereavement literature, see Judith A. Cook, "The Adjustment of Parents Following the Death of a Child from a Terminal

Illness," PhD dissertation, The Ohio State University, Columbus, Ohio, 1982.

12. For a discussion of this phenomenon in terms of marriages, see Levinger, op. cit.

Chapter Nine.   The Future of the Other Woman

1. U. S. Bureau of the Census, *Statistical Abstracts of the United States, 1984* (Washington, D. C.: U. S. Government Printing Office, 1984), Table 51, p. 49.

2. See Noreen Goldman, Charles Westoff, and Charles Hammerslough, "Demography of the Marriage Market in the United States," *Population Index* 50, 1, 1984, pp. 5–25. For a subjective account, see Amanda Spake, "The Choices that Brought Me Here," *MS. Magazine* (November) 1984, pp. 48–52, 138.

3. See Carol Gilligan, *In a Different Voice: Psychological Theory and Women's Development* (Cambridge, Mass.: Harvard V. P., 1982).

4. See Gilligan, op. cit.; Lillian B. Rubin, *Intimate Strangers: Men and Women Together* (New York: Harper, 1983). For a discussion of how the socially structured inequality between the sexes affects their intimate lives, see Laurel (Walum) Richardson, *The Dynamics of Sex and Gender: A Sociological Perspective* (Boston: Houghton, 1981).

5. Emile Durkheim, *Suicide* (New York: Free Press, 1964).

6. Gilbert D. Nass, Roger W. Libby and Mary Pat Fisher, *Sexual Choices* (Belmont, Ca.: Wadsworth, 1981).

7. If a belief or institution plays a major role in keeping the *status quo,* and if that belief or institution is seriously challenged or removed, then alternatives will develop that fulfill the same function. Old ideas will be replaced with seemingly new ones, but the new ones will serve the same master. The *status quo* in all known societies is that which benefits the ruling class; they have a vested interest, whether articulated or not, in maintaining themselves in power, and will consciously and unconsciously support those new cultural items which support their positions.

8. Lenore Weitzman, *Divorce: The Social and Legal Implications for Women and Children* (New York: Free Press, 1985).

9. It is important to note that in this respect the single woman–married man relationship is different from other socially unacceptable relationships. Although gay, interracial, and older woman–younger man relationships, for example, may also be constructed in secrecy, thereby

creating deeper emotional attachments than might otherwise arise, whenever they appear in public they cannot pass as a regular couple, the way a single woman and married man can. Older woman–younger man, same-sex, and different-race couples by their very presence— their undeniable visibility as norm-breaking relationships—strike at social conservatism and the status quo. Relationships between black men and white women, the increasingly more common interracial pattern, and relationships between older women and younger men, moreover, challenge the assumption of male dominance in relationships. In black male–white female relationships and older woman– younger man ones, the male and female are more status equals because of the women's higher racial and age status.

10. Although *some* women have been highly career-oriented in the past, the numbers have been few in contrast to the large-scale possibilities today, possibilities which would not only give the woman greater financial security but could have an impact on the organization of work and the economy. Women can bring with them into managerial and entrepreneurial positions their female socialization to care about personal relationships. The conditions of the workplace might change, reflecting women managers' concerns with reducing stress and using broader criteria for assessing employee productivity (See Anne Statham, "Women and Men Supervisors and Their Secretaries: The Implications of Sex Differences in Managerial Styles," unpublished manuscript, University of Wisconsin-Parkside, 1984.) With more independence in the workplace, women would have greater independence in how to spend their money, including turning to other women for professional advice and services. Women lawyers, financial planners, accountants, stockbrokers, and real-estate agents may be sought out, making the development of a true second economy beside the first one a possibility.

11. If many women do prioritize their relationships with women, children may have many role models of adult women who have lived happily ever after as single women. In consequence, the prestige of the female might be raised in the eyes of the succeeding generation.

Bibliography

ADAMS, VIRGINIA
1982 "Getting at the Heart of Jealous Love." In Robert H. Walsh and Ollie Pocs (eds.), *Marriage and Family 82/83*. Guilford, Conn.: Annual Editions, Dushkin, 39–44.

ALTMAN, MERYL
1984 "Everything They Always Wanted You to Know: The Ideology of Popular Sex." In Carole S. Vance (ed.), *Pleasure and Danger: Exploring Female Sexuality*. Boston: Routledge and Kegan Paul, 115–130.

ATWATER, LYNN
1982 *The Extramarital Connection: Sex, Intimacy, and Identity*. New York: Irvington.

BAETZ, RUTH
1984 "The Coming-Out Process: Violence Against Lesbians." In Trudy Darty and Sandee Potter (eds.), *Women-Identified-Women*. Palo Alto, Ca.: Mayfield, 51–67.

BARKAS, JANET LESS
1983 *Friendship Throughout Life*. New York: Public Affairs Pamphlets.

BARRY, KATHLEEN
1984 "Female Sexual Slavery." In Alison M. Jagger and Paula S. Rothenberg (eds.), *Feminist Frameworks*. New York: McGraw-Hill, 405–416.

BELL, ROBERT R.
1981 *Worlds of Friendship*. Beverly Hills, Ca.: Sage.

Berger, Peter L.
1963   *Invitation to Sociology: A Humanistic Perspective.* Garden City, N.Y.: Doubleday.

Berger, Peter L., and Hans F. Kellner
1964   "Marriage and the Construction of Reality." *Diogenes* 46:1–25.

Berman, Eleanor
1984   "What Working Women Tell Their Therapists." *Working Mother* (March): 29–32.

Bernard, Jessie
1971   "The Paradox of the Happy Marriage." In Vivian Gornick and Barbara Moran (eds.), *Women in Sexist Society: Studies in Power and Powerlessness.* New York: New American, 145–163.
1979   "Foreword." In George Levinger and Oliver C. Moles (eds.), *Divorce and Separation: Context, Causes, and Consequences.* New York: Basic, ix–xv.

Bird, Lois S.
1970   *How to Be a Happily Married Mistress.* Garden City, N. Y.: Doubleday.

Blau, Peter
1964   *Exchange and Power in Social Life.* New York: Wiley.

Blumstein, Phillip, and Pepper Schwartz
1983   *American Couples: Money, Work, Sex.* New York: Morrow.

Bradford, David L., Alice G. Sargent, and Melinda S. Sprague
1980   "The Executive Man and Woman: The Issue of Sexuality." In Dail Ann Neugarten and Jay M. Shafrit (eds.), *Sexuality in Organizations: Romantic and Coercive Behaviors at Work.* Oak Park, Ill.: Moore, 17–28.

Brownstein, Rachel M.
1984   *Becoming a Heroine: Reading about Women in Novels.* New York: Penguin.

Calderone, Mary S.
1984   "Above and Beyond Politics: The Sexual Socialization of Children." In Carole S. Vance (ed.), *Pleasure and Danger: Exploring Female Sexuality.* Boston: Routledge and Kegan Paul, 131–137.

Cargan, Leonard
1982   *Singles: Myths and Realities.* Beverly Hills, Ca.: Sage.

Cassell, Carol
1984   *Swept Away: Why Women Fear Their Own Sexuality.* New York: Simon & Schuster.

Cavan, Sherri
1966   *Liquor License: An Ethnography of Bar Behavior.* Chicago: Aldine.

CHODOROW, NANCY
1978   *The Reproduction of Mothering: Psychoanalysis and the Sociology of Gender.*
Berkeley, Ca.: U. of California P.

COOK, JUDITH A.
1982   "The Adjustment of Parents Following the Death of a Child from
a Terminal Illness." PhD dissertation, The Ohio State University,
Columbus, Ohio.

COZBY, PAUL C.
1973   "Self-Disclosure: A Literature Review." *Psychological Bulletin* 79: 73–
91.

CUNNINGHAM, MARY
1984   *Power Play: What Really Happened at Bendix.* New York: Simon & Schuster.

DANIELS, ARLENE KAPLAN
1967   "The Low-Caste Stranger in Social Research." In Gideon Sjoberg
(ed.), *Ethics, Politics, and Social Research.* Cambridge, Mass.: Schenkman,
267–296.

DIAMOND, JOHN TIMOTHY
1977   "On the Social Structure of Imagery: The Case of Gender." PhD
dissertation, The Ohio State University, Columbus, Ohio.
1983   "Caring Work." *Contemporary Sociology* 13: 556–558.

DIIORIO, JUDITH A.
1982   "Nomad Vans and Lady Vanners: A Critical Feminist Analysis
of a Van Club." PhD dissertation, The Ohio State University, Columbus, Ohio.

DOUDNA, CHRISTINE (WITH FERN MCBRIDE)
1981   "Where Are the Men for the Women at the Top." In Peter Stein
(ed.), *Single Life: Unmarried Adults in Social Context,* New York: St.
Martin's, 21–34.

EHRENREICH, BARBARA
1983   *The Hearts of Men: American Dreams and the Flight from Commitment.* Garden City, N. Y.: Doubleday.

EICHLER, MARGRIT
1980   *The Double Standard: A Feminist Critique of Feminist Social Science.* New
York: St. Martin's.

ELBAUM, PHILLIP L.
1981   "The Dynamics, Implications, and Treatment of Extramarital Sexual Relationships for the Family Therapist." *Journal of Marital and
Family Therapy* 7: 489–495.

EPSTEIN, CYNTHIA
1970 *Women's Place: Options and Limits on a Professional Career.* Berkeley, Ca.:
       U. of California P.

ESKAPA, SHIRLEY
1984 *Woman Versus Woman: The Extramarital Affair.* New York: Franklin
       Watts.

GARFINKEL, HAROLD
1968 *Studies in Ethnomethodology.* Englewood Cliffs, N. J.: Prentice-Hall.

GILLESPIE, DAIR L.
1971 "Who Has the Power? The Marital Struggle." *Journal of Marriage
       and the Family* 33:445–458.

GILLIGAN, CAROL
1982 *In a Different Voice: Psychological Theory and Women's Development.* Cam-
       bridge, Mass.: Harvard U. P.

GLASER, BARNEY G., AND ANSELM STRAUSS
1967 *The Discovery of Grounded Theory: Strategies for Qualitative Research.* Chi-
       cago: Aldine.

GOFFMAN, ERVING
1963 *Stigma: Notes on the Management of Spoiled Identity.* Englewood Cliffs,
       N. J.: Prentice-Hall.
1976 *Gender Advertisements.* New York: Harper.

GOLDMAN, NOREEN, CHARLES WESTOFF, AND CHARLES HAMMERSLOUGH
1984 "Demography of the Marriage Market in the United States." *Popula-
       tion Index* 50, 1:5–25.

GORDON, MICHAEL, AND PENELOPE SHANKWEILER
1971 "Different Equals Less: Female Sexuality in Recent Marriage Manu-
       als." *Journal of Marriage and the Family* 33:459–466.

GRAUERHOLZ, ELIZABETH
1983 "Initiation and Response: The Dynamics of Sexual Interaction."
       Unpublished paper, Indiana University, Bloomington, Ind.

GUTTENTAG, MARCIA, AND PAUL SECORD
1983 *Too Many Women? The Sex Ratio Question.* Beverly Hills: Sage.

HACKER, ANDREW, EDITOR
1983 *U/S: A Statistical Portrait of the American People.* New York: Viking.

HENLEY, NANCY M.
1977 *Body Politics: Power, Sex, and Nonverbal Communication.* Englewood Cliffs,
       N. J.: Prentice-Hall.

HESS, BETH B.
1981 "Friendship and Gender Roles over the Life Course." In Peter Stein
       (ed.), *Single Life: Unmarried Adults in Social Context.* New York: St.
       Martin's, 104–115.

HESS, BETH B., ELIZABETH W. MARKSON, AND PETER STEIN
1985 *Sociology.* New York: Macmillan.

HILL, CHARLES T., ZICK RUBIN, AND LETITIA ANNE PEPLAU
1979 "Breakups Before Marriage: The End of 103 Affairs." In George Levinger and Oliver C. Moles (eds.), *Divorce and Separation: Context, Causes, and Consequences.* New York: Basic, 64–82.

HOCHSCHILD, ARLIE RUSSELL
1983 *The Managed Heart: Commercialization of Human Feeling.* Berkeley: U. of California P.

HUBER, JOAN
1983 "Ambiguities in Identity Transformation: From Sugar and Spice to Professor." In Laurel Richardson and Verta Taylor (eds.), *Feminist Frontiers: Rethinking Sex, Gender, and Society.* Boston, Mass.: Addison-Wesley, 330–337.

HUBER, JOAN, AND GLENNA SPITZE
1983 *Sex Stratification: Children, Housework, Jobs.* New York: Academic.

JOURARD, SIDNEY M.
1964 *The Transparent Self.* New York: Van Nostrand.
1971 *Self-Disclosure: An Experimental Analysis of the Transparent Self.* New York: Wiley-Interscience.

KALMUSS, DEBRA, AND MURRAY STRAUS
1982 "Wives' Marital Dependency and Wife Abuse." *Journal of Marriage and the Family* 44:277–286.

KING, KARL, JACK O. BALSWICK, AND IRA E. ROBINSON
1977 "The Continuing Premarital Sexual Revolution Among College Females." *Journal of Marriage and the Family* (August): 455–459.

KORDA, MICHAEL
1973 *Male Chauvinism: How It Works.* New York: Random.

LATANÉ, Bibb, and John M. Darley
1969 "Bystander Apathy." *American Scientist* 57:224–268.

LAWS, JUDITH LONG, AND PEPPER SCHWARTZ
1977 *Sexual Scripts: The Social Construction of Female Sexuality.* Hinsdale, Ill.: Dryden.

LEMKAU, JEANNE PARR
1979 "Personality and Background Characteristics of Women in Male-Dominated Occupations: A Review." *Psychology of Women Quarterly* 4(2):221–240.

LESTER, MARILYN
1979 "Making Music Together: A Sociological Formulation of Intimate Encounters Between Males and Females." Presented to the American Sociological Association Meetings, Boston, Mass.

LEVER, JANET
1976 "Sex Differences in the Games Children Play." *Social Problems* 23:478–487.
1978 "Sex Differences in the Complexity of Children's Play and Games." *American Sociological Review* 43:471–483.

LEVINGER, GEORGE
1979 "A Social Psychological Perspective on Marital Dissolution." In George Levinger and Oliver C. Moles (eds.), *Divorce and Separation: Context, Causes, and Consequences.* New York: Basic, 37–60.

LEVINSON, DANIEL J.
1978 *The Seasons of a Man's Life.* New York: Knopf.

LIBBY, ROGER W.
1977 "Extramarital and Comarital Sex: A Critique of the Literature." In Roger W. Libby and Robert N. Whitehurst (eds.), *Marriage and Its Alternatives: Exploring Intimate Life Styles.* Glencoe, Ill.: Scott Foresman, 80–111.

LIPMAN-BLUMEN, JEAN
1984 *Gender Roles and Power.* Englewood Cliffs, N. J.: Prentice-Hall.

McCLELLAND, DAVID C.
1975 *Power: The Inner Experience.* New York: Irvington.

MacKINNON, CATHERINE A.
1979 *Sexual Harassment of Working Women: A Case of Sex Discrimination.* New Haven, Conn.: Yale U. P.

MENAGHAN, ELIZABETH G.
1983 "Individual Coping Efforts: Moderators of the Relationship Between Life Stress and Mental Health Outcomes." In Howard B. Kaplan (ed.), *Psychological Stress: Trends in Theory and Research.* New York: Academic, 157–189.

MERTON, ROBERT K.
1957 *Social Theory and Social Structure.* New York: Free Press.

MOOS, RUDOLPH H., AND ANDREW G. BILLINGS
1982 "Conceptualizing and Measuring Coping Resources and Processes." In Leo Goldberger and Shlomo Breznitz (eds.), *Handbook of Stress: Theoretical and Clinical Aspects.* New York: Free Press, 212–230.

MORGAN, MARABEL
1973 *The Total Woman.* New York: Pocket Books.

NASS, GILBERT D., ROGER W. LIBBY, AND MARY PAT FISHER
1981 *Sexual Choices.* Belmont, Ca.: Wadsworth.

NEUGARTEN, DAIL ANN, AND JAY M. SHAFRITZ, EDITORS
1980 *Sexuality in Organizations: Romantic and Coercive Behaviors at Work.* Oak Park, Ill.: Moore.

NORTH, MAURICE, AND FREDERICK TAOLES
1977 "Is Adultery Biological?" *New Society* 21, 772:125–126.

PATTERSON, JOAN M., AND HAMILTON I. MCCUBBIN
1984 "Gender Roles and Coping." *Journal of Marriage and the Family* 46:95–104.

PHILLIPS, JOHN A.
1984 *Eve: The History of an Idea.* New York: Harper.

PIETROPINTO, ANTHONY, AND JACQUELINE SIMENAUR
1977 *Beyond the Male Myth.* New York: New American Library.

REISS, IRA L.
1960 *Premarital Sexual Standards in America.* New York: Free Press.
1980 *Family Systems in America,* 3rd ed. New York: Holt.

REISS, IRA L., AND BRENT C. MILLER
1979 "Heterosexual Permissiveness: A Theoretical Analysis." In Wesley R. Burr, Reuben Hill, Ivan Nye, and Ira L. Reiss (eds.), *Contemporary Theories about the Family,* Vol. 1. New York: Free Press, 57–100.

REISS, IRA L., R. E. ANDERSON, AND G. C. SPONAUGLE
1980 "A Multivariate Model of the Determinants of Extramarital Sexual Permissiveness." *Journal of Marriage and the Family* 42:395–411.

RICH, ADRIENNE
1980 "Compulsory Heterosexuality and Lesbian Existence." *Signs* 5 (Summer):631–660.

RICHARDSON, LAUREL (WALUM)
1979 "The 'Other Woman': The End of the Long Affair." *Alternative Lifestyles* 2:397–414.
1981 *The Dynamics of Sex and Gender: A Sociological Perspective.* Boston, Mass.: Houghton.

RICHARDSON, LAUREL, AND VERTA TAYLOR, EDITORS
1983 *Feminist Frontiers: Rethinking Sex, Gender, and Society.* Boston, Mass.: Addison-Wesley.

ROBERTSON, IAN
1977 *Sociology.* New York: Worth.

RUBIN, LILLIAN B.
1983 *Intimate Strangers: Men and Women Together.* New York: Harper.

RUBIN, ZICK
1974 "Lovers and Other Strangers: The Development of Intimacy in Encounters and Relationships." *American Scientist* 62:182–190.

RUDDICK, SARA, AND PAMELA DANIEL, EDITORS
1977 *Working It Out.* New York: Pantheon.

Safilios-Rothschild, Constantina
1977   *Love, Sex, and Sex Roles.* Englewood Cliffs, N. J.: Prentice-Hall.

Saluter, Arlene
1983   "Marital Status and Living Arrangements: March, 1983." *Current Population Reports, Population Characteristics.* Series P-20, No. 389, issued June, 1983. Washington, D. C.: Bureau of the Census.

Sands, Melissa
1981   "When Women Have Affairs . . . Myths About 'Mistresses'." *MS. Magazine* (November): 116.

SanGiovanni, Lucinda
1978   *Ex-Nuns: A Study of Emergent Role Passage.* Norwood, N. J.: Ablex.

Sarsby, Jacqueline
1983   *Romantic Love and Society: Its Place in the Modern World.* New York: Penguin.

Schur, Edwin M.
1984   *Labeling Women Deviant: Gender, Stigma, and Social Control.* New York: Random.

Sheehy, Gail
1976   *Passages: Predictable Crises of Adult Life.* New York: Dutton.

Simenauer, Jacqueline, and David Carroll
1982   *Singles: The New Americans.* New York: New American Library.

Simmel, Georg
1950   *The Sociology of Georg Simmel.* Trans. and ed. Kurt H. Wolff. New York: Free Press.

Snitow, Ann, Christine Stansall, and Sharon Thompson, editors
1983   *Powers of Desire: The Politics of Sexuality.* New York: Monthly Review Press.

Spake, Amanda
1984   "The Choices that Brought Me Here." *MS. Magazine* (November):48–52, 138.

Spanier, Graham B., and Randie L. Margolis
1983   "Marital Separation and Extramarital Sexual Behavior." *The Journal of Sex Research* 19:23–48.

Statham, Anne
1984   "Women and Men Supervisors and Their Secretaries: The Implications of Sex Differences in Managerial Styles." Unpublished manuscript, University of Wisconsin-Parkside.

Statham, Anne (Macke), and Laurel Richardson (with Judith A. Cook)
1980   *Sex-Typed Teaching Styles of University Professors and Student Reactions.* Washington, D. C.: National Institute of Education.

STEIN, PETER
1981 "Understanding Single Adulthood." In Peter Stein (ed.), *Single Life: Unmarried Adults in Social Context.* New York: St. Martin's, 9–21.

STRAUS, MURRAY, RICHARD GELLES, AND SUSAN STEINMETZ
1980 *Behind Closed Doors: Violence in the American Family.* Garden City, N. Y.: Doubleday.

STREAN, HERBERT S.
1980 *The Extramarital Affair.* New York: Free Press.

STRYKER, SHELDON
1980 *Symbolic Interactionism: A Social Structural Version.* Menlo Park, Ca.: Benjamin/Cummings.

STRYKER, SHELDON, AND ANNE STATHAM
1985 "Symbolic Interaction and Role Theory." In Gardner Linzey (ed.), *Handbook of Social Psychology.* Forthcoming.

SWAIN, SCOTT O.
1984 "Male Intimacy in Same-Sex Friendship: The Impact of Gender-Validating Activities." Presented to the American Sociological Association Meetings, San Francisco.

SWIDLER, ANN
1980 "Love and Adulthood in American Culture." In Neil Smelser and Erik Eriksen (eds.), *Theories of Work and Love in America,* Cambridge, Mass.: Harvard U. P. 120–147.

TAYLOR, VERTA
1983 "The Future of Feminism in the 1980s: A Social Movement Analysis." In Laurel Richardson and Verta Taylor (eds.), *Feminist Frontiers: Rethinking Sex, Gender, and Society.* Boston, Mass.: Addison-Wesley, 434–451.

THOMAS, KEITH
1980 *Religion and the Decline of Magic.* New York: Penguin.

THOMPSON, ANTHONY B.
1983 "Extramarital Sex: A Review of the Research Literature." *The Journal of Sex Research* 19, 1:1–22.

U. S. BUREAU OF THE CENSUS
1984 *Statistical Abstracts of the United States, 1984.* Washington, D. C.: U. S. Government Printing Office.

VANCE, CAROLE S., EDITOR
1984 *Pleasure and Danger: Exploring Female Sexuality.* Boston: Routledge and Kegan Paul.

WALSTER, ELAINE G., WILLIAM WALSTER, JANE PILIAVIN, AND LYNN SCHMIDT
1973 "Playing Hard to Get: Understanding an Elusive Phenomenon." *Journal of Personality and Social Psychology* 26, 2:113–121.

WEITZMAN, LENORE
1985   *Divorce: Social and Economic Implications for Women and Children.* New York: Free Press.

WEST, CANDACE
1979   "Against Our Will: Male Interruptions of Female Conversations in Cross-Sex Conversation." In Judith Orasnu, Mariam K. Slater, and Lenore Loeb Adler (eds.), *Language, Sex, and Gender: Does La Différence Make a Difference?* New York: New York Academy of Sciences Annals, 81–100.

WISEMAN, JACQUELINE
1976   "Sex as a Personal and Social Phenomenon." In Jacqueline P. Wiseman (ed.), *The Social Psychology of Sex.* New York: Harper, 10–16.

WRIGHT, PAUL H.
1982   "Men's Friendships, Women's Friendships, and the Alleged Inferiority of the Latter." *Sex Roles* 8:1–21.

YABLONSKY, LEWIS
1979   *The Extra-Sex Factor.* New York: Times.

ZATZ, JUDITH MILSTEIN
1976   "How Do You Love Me? Let Me Count the Ways (The Phenomenology of Being Loved)." *Sociological Inquiry* 46:17–22.

ZETTERBERG, HANS L.
1966   "The Secret Ranking." *Journal of Marriage and the Family* 28, 2:161–166.

Index